SOCRATIC SEMINARS IN THE BLOCK

Wanda H. Ball

and

Pam Brewer

EYE ON EDUCATION
6 DEPOT WAY WEST, SUITE 106
LARCHMONT, NY 10538
(914) 833–0551
(914) 833–0761 fax

Library of Congress Cataloging-in-Publication Data

Ball, Wanda H., 1953–
    Socratic seminars in the block / by Wand H. Ball and Pam Brewer.
        p.   cm.
    ISBN 1-883001-79-X
        1. Questioning.   2. Lesson planning.   I. Brewer, Pam, 1952–
II. Title.
LB1027.44.B35   2000
371.3'7—dc21   99–32739
                                                                        CIP

10 9 8 7 6 5 4 3 2 1

Editorial and production services provided by
Richard H. Adin Freelance Editorial Services,
52 Oakwood Blvd., Poughkeepsie, NY 12603
(914-471-3566)

Also Available from EYE ON EDUCATION

Teaching in the Block:
Strategies for Engaging Active Learners
edited by Robert Lynn Canady and Michael D. Rettig

Encouraging Student Engagement in the Block Period
by David Marshak

Questions and Answers About Block Scheduling
by Donald Gainey and John Brucato

Supervision and Staff Development in the Block
by Sally J. Zepeda and R. Stewart Mayers

Teaching Mathematics in the Block
by Susan Gilkey and Carla Hunt

Supporting Students with Learning Needs in the Block
by Marcia Conti-D'Antonio, Robert Bertrando, and Joanne Eisenberger

Teaching Foreign Languages in the Block
by Deborah Blaz

Action Research on Block Scheduling
by David Marshak

The 4x4 Block Schedule
by J. Allen Queen and Kimberly G. Isenhouer

The Paideia Classroom:
Teaching for Understanding
by Terry Roberts with Laura Billings

The Interdisciplinary Curriculum
by Arthur K. Ellis and Carol J. Stuen

Writing in the Content Areas
by Amy Benjamin

Performance Standards and Authentic Learning
by Allan A. Glatthorn

Performance Assessment and Standards-Based Curricula:
The Achievement Cycle
by Allan A. Glatthorn

Coaching and Mentoring First-Year and Student Teachers
by India Podsen and Vicki Denmark

Best Practices from America's Middle Schools
by Charles R. Watson

The Performance Assessment Handbook:
Volume 1: Portfolios and Socratic Seminars
Volume 2: Performances and Exhibitions
by Bil Johnson

The School Portfolio:
A Comprehensive Framework for School Improvement, 2nd ed.
by Victoria L. Bernhardt

Data Analysis for Comprehensive Schoolwide Improvement
by Victoria L. Bernhardt

Research on Educational Innovations, 2nd ed.
by Arthur K. Ellis and Jeffrey T. Fouts

Transforming Schools into Community Learning Centers
by Steve R. Parson

A Collection of Performance Tasks and Rubrics
Primary School Mathematics
by Charlotte Danielson and Pia Hansen

Middle School Mathematics
by Charlotte Danielson

Upper Elementary School Mathematics
by Charlotte Danielson

High School Mathematics
by Charlotte Danielson and Elizabeth Marquez

The Educator's Brief Guide to the Internet and the World Wide Web
by Eugene F. Provenzo, Jr.

Instruction and the Learning Environment
by James Keefe and John Jenkins

Foreign Language Teacher's Guide to Active Learning
by Deborah Blaz

Directory of Programs for Students at Risk
by Thomas L. Williams

Staff Development:
Practices that Promote Leadership in Learning Communities
by Sally J. Zepeda

FOREWORD

Block schedules provide opportunities for teachers to change their instructional strategies so that students become more active and successful learners. There is a growing body of evidence from experiences with high school block scheduling that strongly supports the notion that with proper staff development and careful schedule design the overall school environment becomes more positive and productive. There is also evidence that many teachers increase their personal contacts with students. Furthermore, when curricular and instructional issues are addressed appropriately, achievement in many schools improves, as measured by factors such as reduced failure rates, increased number of students on honor rolls, and higher test scores.

Because we believe that instructional change is the key to successful block scheduling, we are sponsoring this series of books, written primarily by teachers who have been successful in teaching in block schedules. While we believe this series can be helpful to teachers working in any type of schedule, the ideas should be especially useful for middle and high school teachers who are "Teaching in the Block."

The idea of scheduling middle and high schools in some way other than daily, single periods is not new. We find in educational history numerous attempts to modify traditional schedules and to give the instructional school day greater flexibility. In the 1960s, for example, approximately 15% of American high schools implemented modular scheduling, which typically combined "mods" of time to create schedules with instructional periods that varied in length from between 15 minutes to classes of 100 minutes or more.

Many reasons have been given for the demise of modular scheduling as practiced during the 1960s and 1970s. However, two of the primary reasons often cited are that (1) too much independent study time was included in those schedules and school management became a problem, and (2) teachers in many schools did not receive training designed to assist them in altering instruction in the longer class period (Canady and Rettig, 1995, pp. 13–15). Current models of block scheduling do not include significant built-in independent study time and, therefore, school management problems are not exacerbated, but helped. We have found, however, that in schools where block scheduling has been implemented successfully, considerable attention has been paid to adapting instruction to maximize the potential of available time.

We repeatedly have stated that if schools merely "change their bells," block scheduling should not be implemented. We also have contended that if teachers are not provided with extensive staff development, block scheduling will be a problem. "The success or failure of the [current] block scheduling movement will be determined largely by the ability of teachers...to improve instruction. Regardless of a school's time schedule, what happens between individual teachers and students in classrooms is still most important, and simply altering the manner in which we schedule school will not ensure better instruction by teachers or increased learning by students" (Canady and Rettig, 1995, p. 240).

In this volume, Wanda H. Ball and Pam F. Brewer explain how teachers can plan and implement Socratic Seminars, a strategy that is particularly appropriate for teaching in a block schedule. In Socratic Seminars, opportunities are provided for students to explore ideas in a supportive environment. During seminar students talk primarily with each other, not just with the teacher; it is the students who "own" the discussion. Students establish an emotional connection to the content selected for a particular lesson and experience the freedom to explore concepts and issues that are directly meaningful to them. We believe this type of "connection" is an important step in helping students later become motivated to express their ideas in a written format. If a seminar is conducted before a writing activity is assigned, often the quality of the students' writing will improve dramatically.

We all have noticed that some students seem to "tune out" when teaching strategies revolve around passive reading or listening. Students tend to be more focused and motivated when they are engaged actively in discussion and when they are talking to and teaching each other. It is important to note, however, that Socratic Seminars are more than typical classroom discussions. Seminars are fine-tuned, teacher-orchestrated procedures which build student motivation and interest in various types of content. Although teachers of mathematics report they use the seminars for a few selected topics, we have found that teachers of the following disciplines most value the Socratic Seminar strategy: English, foreign languages, social studies, and some science teachers.

Ball and Brewer demonstrate that a successful Socratic Seminar requires more from teachers than merely leading a discussion group. Setting up and maintaining the appropriate environment for a seminar requires time, a commodity often not available in traditional schedules. The extended time block typically found in 4/4 semester schedules, trimester schedules and A/B alternating-day schedules provides the time for teachers to implement the Socratic Seminar effectively.

The authors of this volume are experienced classroom teachers who have trained hundreds of teachers to make Socratic Seminars work. They have included suggested ideas for formulating "good seminar questions," and appropriate follow-up writing activities, as well as structures for assessing seminars. We recommend this book highly for middle and high school teachers who are working in a block schedule. Both students and teachers will be rewarded if the ideas and strategies in this book are adopted.

Robert Lynn Canady
Michael D. Rettig

PREFACE

Socratic Seminars in the Block was written with three goals in mind: First, we wanted teachers to value the seminar as a particularly useful strategy for student ownership and motivation in extended blocks of time. Second, we wanted to give teachers practical guidelines, pedagogy, and forms to implement the seminar into their disciplines. Third, we wanted evaluators to understand how the seminar may fit into teacher appraisal.

Chapter 1 explores the historical and philosophical base of the Socratic seminar and how the strategy is especially suited to block scheduling. In Chapter 2, we provide the nuts and bolts on how to lead a seminar, including specific student behaviors, teacher behaviors and the rules of engagement. Chapter 3 prepares the classroom and reader for the seminar experience with the logistics of classroom management and techniques and models to prepare student participants.

Before the seminar can begin, appropriate texts are needed. Chapter 4 examines the litmus test for good texts and offers a sample bibliography. Applications to disciplines are the focus in Chapter 5. Here, models are provided for integrating seminars among several disciplines. In Chapter 6, "Writing Seminar Questions," the importance of question development is explained and modeled. Strong questioning techniques are essential to successful seminars.

Lesson design using seminar in a block schedule is addressed in Chapter 7, in which planning logs, time sequences, seminar tasks, and four model lessons are available. Chapter 8 responds to questions typically asked by teachers to help them avoid the pitfalls that may sabotage a seminar.

The importance of assessing seminar and models for assessment are presented in Chapter 9. Seminar leaders are encouraged to view the assessment chapter as a guide for developing their own assessment practices as opposed to a "turn key" antidote for grading. Chapter 10 provides reassurances to teachers who are incorporating seminar into lesson plans. Directed toward administrators and teacher evaluators, appraisal of seminar is explored and a model evaluation form is provided.

While the "tools" are given in *Socratic Seminars in the Block*, teachers are urged to attend workshops to practice their skills and experience the process as both a participant and facilitator.

Wanda H. Ball
Pam Brewer

ABOUT THE AUTHORS

Wanda H. Ball, a native of Grundy, Virginia, is in her twentieth year of teaching. She has taught in Virginia, Maryland, and North Carolina in grades 5–12. During the past 9 years, she has actively used the seminar strategy in her classroom at Person High School in Roxboro, North Carolina, and conducted model seminars with elementary, middle school, and high school students. In 1992, she was the recipient of the Stovall Excellence in Education Award for Innovative Teaching.

She is the coauthor, with Pam Brewer, of the Socratic Seminar chapter in Canady and Rettig's *Teaching in the Block: Strategies for Engaging Active Learners*, and her class is featured in the October 1994 issue of *The Video Journal of Education*. Ball received her initial training at the National Paideia Center at the University of North Carolina at Chapel Hill, and is a 1976 graduate of Berea College with a B.A. in English Education. She is married and has one son, Bryce.

Ball may be reached at Person High School, 1010 Ridge Road, Roxboro, NC 27573 or by e-mail at whball@person.net.

A North Carolina native, **Pam Brewer** is a 14-year veteran high school teacher of English, journalism, and drama. For the past 10 years, Brewer has served as Assistant Principal for Instruction at Person High School in Roxboro, North Carolina. A former North Carolina Teacher of the Year, Brewer has presented many workshops on the topics of school reform, high school block scheduling, successful strategies for teaching in the 90-minute block, and Socratic questioning through seminars. She has trained district staff in implementing the effective schools process, learning styles research, and Socratic Seminar. In 1993, Brewer led Person High School's successful restructuring to a 4/4 block schedule.

Brewer coauthored, with Wanda Ball, the Socratic Seminar chapter in Canady and Rettig's *Teaching in the Block: Strategies for Engaging Active Learners*, and her work was featured in *Video Journal*'s production, "High School Alternative Scheduling" (vol. 4, issue 2). She is a Meredith College graduate and holds a masters degree in English from North Carolina State University and principal's certification from the University of North Carolina at Chapel Hill.

Brewer can be contacted at Person High School, 1010 Ridge Road, Roxboro, NC 27573, or by e-mail at pbrewer@person.net.

TABLE OF CONTENTS

FOREWORD v
PREFACE vii
ABOUT THE AUTHORS viii

1 FROM SOCRATES TO SEMINARS 1
    Socrates the Teacher 2
    Seminar as Sound Practice 3
        Community 4
        Connection 4
        Communication 4
        Control 5
    Block Scheduling and Socratic Seminar 5
    References 7

2 ROLES, RULES, AND RESPONSIBILITIES DURING A SEMINAR 9
    Snapshot of a Socratic Seminar 11
    Student Responsibilities and Rules During Seminar 13
        Thinking During Seminar 14
        Speaking During Seminar 15
        Listening During Seminar 15
        Self-Awareness During Seminar 15
    Seminars With At-Risk Students 17
    Teacher Responsibilities and Rules During Seminar 17
    References 20

3 PREPARING THE CLASSROOM AND READER FOR SOCRATIC
    SEMINARS 21
    Preparing the Classroom for Socratic Seminars 21
        Inner/Outer Circles 22
            Outer Circle Considerations 23
            Benefits of the Inner/Outer Circle Format 24
    Preparing the Reader for Seminar 27
    Directed Reading for Seminar 27
        Directed Reading Activity Model 29
        Three-Level Study Guides 31
        Marking a Text 37
        Graphic Organizer Models 37
        Student Reading Guides 40
    References 40

4 TEXT SELECTION. **41**
Guidelines for Determining the Suitability of Texts 41
Strategies for Text Selection 42
    Combined Readings 43
    Using Artworks as Texts. 44
    Using Films as Texts 44
    Math Texts. 46
Sources of Seminar Texts. 46

5 APPLYING SEMINARS TO THE DISCIPLINES. **51**
Suggestions for an Integrated Seminar Unit. 53
    History. 53
    Science 54
    English 57
    Additional Seminar Suggestions 57
    Various Ways a Single Text May Be Applied to
        Different Disciplines 58

6 WRITING SOCRATIC QUESTIONS **61**
Opening Questions. 61
Core Questions 63
Closing Questions 64
Followup Questions 65
Developing Seminar Questions 67

7 LESSON DESIGN USING SEMINARS **77**
Planning in the Block. 77
Planning the Socratic Seminar 82
    Preseminar Planning 83
    Postseminar Planning 91
Model Lesson Plans. 100
    Model Lesson 1: "This Sacred Soil" 100
    Model Lesson 2: "The Frogs Desiring a King" 106
    Model Lesson 3: "A Psalm of Life" 111
    Model Lesson 4: "Self-Reliance" 116

8 TROUBLESHOOTING THE "WHAT IFS...". **123**
What if the Opening Question Is Asked and No One Responds? 123
What If Some Students Do Not "Qualify" for Seminar? 124
What if a Student Misbehaves During Seminar? 125
What if One Student Tries to Dominate the Seminar?. 125
What if Some Students Do Not Speak at All During Seminar? 126
What if Some Students Think of Things after Seminar
    They Wish They had Said? 126
What if Students Go Off on a Line of Reasoning that Is
    Faulty or Inaccurate and Start Building on It? 127

What if Class Ends and the Seminar Is Not Finished? 127
What if Some Students Are Absent and Miss a Seminar?. 128

9 ASSESSMENT OF SEMINARS. **129**
Recording Student Behaviors 130
Charting 130
Checklists 131
Assigning Point Values 132
Assessment Models. 133
Grading Feedback. 133
Assessment of Preseminars and Postseminars. 146
Grading Challenges and Wrapup 151

10 PROFESSIONAL EVALUATION AND COACHING FOR SEMINAR . . **153**
The Bottom Line. 159

BIBLIOGRAPHY **161**

1

FROM SOCRATES TO SEMINARS

"Something old, something new...."

Innovative and ancient, the Socratic Seminar is an exciting and effective strategy, for all grades K–12, for provoking student thought and dialogue, and for ownership of learning. It is a unique alternative to traditional class discussions because in Seminar, students speak 97% of class time.

In this kind of seminar, participants sit in a circle, and, prompted by their teacher's open-ended, provocative questions, engage each other in thoughtful dialogue. Their subject is a shared reading, chosen for its richness of ideas and issues. Students are responsible for talking primarily with each other, not with the teacher, who facilitates and clarifies through questioning, but who never contributes to the discussion. Often, when students become deeply engaged in the discussion, 55 minutes isn't enough time; therefore, the strategy lends itself well to school schedules built for longer blocks of time.

The great philosopher and moral teacher, Socrates, had no competency goals, organized curriculum, or even license to teach. He certainly never took the NTE. Yet when he walked and talked with the young men of Athens 2400 years ago, he inspired awe and ire with his unconventional teaching practices. His approach was to take a subject—an idea, statement, or argument of his day—and then raise thoughtful questions, without proposing to have any wise answers himself. This deliberate and repeated probing of his students' thought would lead, he hoped, to their self-knowledge and understanding and ultimately to the establishment of truth.

In 1982, Mortimer Adler returned to Socratic questioning in *The Paideia Proposal*, one of three "columns" for learning. He suggested that didactic instruction, coaching, and exercises are appropriate methodology for the goals of gaining specific content (the facts) and skill building (the practice). But he highlighted Socratic questioning in a class seminar for reaching the third goal: exploring and understanding the ideas and issues surrounding content (the enlarged understanding).

1

SOCRATES THE TEACHER

So what was Socrates onto? And why would teachers find a modern manifestation of some of his elements not only refreshing and fun, but also good practice that is responsive to the most recent knowledge about how thinking, learning, and retention occur.

"Know thyself!" is the pronouncement carved onto the Temple of Apollo at Delphi. In Plato's *Apology*, the oracle drives Socrates, who proclaims, "God orders me to fulfill the philosopher's mission of searching into myself and other men,…" though, he claims, "I know that I have no wisdom, small or great." This directive to search for self leads him to one who had a keen reputation for wisdom, a respected politician. Yet, in examining him, Socrates finds him wanting. He proves not to be wise at all; Socrates tells him so and then leaves musing:

> Although I do not suppose that either of us knows anything beautiful or good, I am better off than he is, for he knows nothing and thinks that he knows; I neither know nor think that I know. I seem to have slightly the advantage.

Only from a start point of "I do not know" can the search for knowledge begin. As a teacher, Socrates knew much but practiced the "ask but do not tell" policy, protesting that he knew "nothing," thus enabling his students to explore their thoughts without his corrective lens.

Another element of his philosophy is his life's quest in pursuit of goodness, beauty, and an explanation of human excellence. This better life is achieved only through knowledge and a search for truth. In the *Apology*, he explains to his friends why he has been unable to hold his tongue, an act that could have saved his life. His mission has been this:

> daily to discourse about virtue, and of those other things about which you hear me examining myself and others, is the greatest good of man…the unexamined life is not worth living.

This philosophy of inquiry searches into good, discovering the energy of a better life. It is a call not to be denied.

As a teacher, Socrates sees himself as a kind of midwife, his mother's actual profession, whereby ideas of his students are either born or stillborn, or aborted if they are "false images." He questions others but offers no answers himself, being their catalyst only in such a way that by association with him, others make profound progress. In "Theaetetus," he explains his art:

> And it is clear that they do this, not because they have ever learned anything from me, but because they have found in themselves many beautiful things and have brought them forth. But the delivery is due to God and me.

He then examines Theaetetus again, "And so...tell us what knowledge is. And never say that you are unable to do so, for if God wills it and gives you courage, you will be able."

With pointed and open-ended questions, Socrates keeps the youth thinking, pondering, exploring, and defending, usually until they give a full account of themselves. In Plato's dialogue *Laches*, Nicias explains the process:

> You seem to me not to be aware that whoever comes nearest to Socrates and enters into conversation with him is liable to be drawn round and round by him in the course of the argument—no matter on what subject it began—not stopping until he is led into giving an account of himself, of how he spends his day, and of the kind of life he has lived in the past; and once he has been entangled in that, Socrates will not let him go until he has thoroughly and properly put all his ways to the test.

And when the questioning is over, the hope is that self-knowledge and understanding would result. In the *Cratylus*, Hermogenus looks for an answer from Socrates who reminds him, "I do not know, but would join you in looking for the truth."

What an inspiration and revelation to teachers that we invite our students to look for truths, to put a spotlight on knowledge, urging young people to think through ideas and issues and to establish and defend positions. And the marvelously manipulative key, it seems, to Socrates' success, other than his professed divine inspiration, is his claim to have no wisdom. How freeing it must have been to thinking minds to hear powerful questions like "What is an examined life?" or "Is it possible to examine everything in one's life?" or "Is living an examined life always desirable?" with the teacher claiming to have no answer, only more questions to help students frame their thinking.

SEMINAR AS SOUND PRACTICE

It is well known that learning is facilitated by the absence of fear, risk, and judgment (Kohn, 1993). The elimination of outward teacher judgment in a managed, risk-free setting such as Socratic Seminars fits nicely with the "rediscovery" that learning thrives in such an environment. The image of the teacher as midwife—assisting with the delivery but absolutely not having the baby—is a rich one that supports the most current strategies of our profession that make students active, not passive, participants in their learning.

Socratic Seminars return ownership for learning to students as they explore a reading, back up their opinions with textual evidence, challenge each other's views, and, most importantly, find, articulate, and develop their "voice." Just as Eudora Welty writes in *One Writer's Beginnings* of the importance of an author finding his voice, young people gain confidence as they direct the discussion, listen to their peers, and hear their own intelligent thoughts. They find a voice.

Sometimes they and their teachers are surprised by the insights that emerge and the learning that takes place.

High retention rates are likewise linked with strategies that have students speaking with each other about content. *The Learning Pyramid* and many other retention studies point to the relatively low (5–20%) return on passive reading or listening to lecture compared to the relatively high (50–90%) retention when students are actively engaged in discussion groups, in teaching others, or in otherwise speaking with their peers. In discussions, cooperative learning groups, pairs, or Socratic Seminars, teachers get off the stage. These strategies prove highly effective as long as the rules of engagement for student exchanges promote individual accountability.

Why does increased retention dovetail with instructional strategies that require students to talk with each other? First, let's accept that community, connection, communication, and control are core human needs. Then let's add that young people tuning in to their peers almost exclusively is developmentally appropriate. Does it not then make sense that greater learning takes place in structures that acknowledge their humanity and harness the academic power of their strongest influence, their peers?

COMMUNITY

Dunn and Dunn (1992) and other studies have repeatedly urged the pair, team, or group dynamic as an attendant factor for learning for some children, particularly those identified as at-risk learners. There is a move toward smaller "Learning Communities" in schools, particularly as buildings get larger at the same time that more needs are identified. Commutes get longer, and students more and more need a social anchor at school. Seminar classes contribute to this sense as students talk and get to know each other on more substantial levels.

CONNECTION

Linking existing knowledge bases with new knowledge naturally occurs in seminar as students become the sense makers. It is not unusual for a student to draw an inference between what is being discussed today with a seminar from last month or even last year, or to see a connection between today's reading and today's news.

COMMUNICATION

If the predominant communication skills are reading, writing, listening, and speaking, which are most used to assess what students know? The obvious answer is reading and writing. And yet what developed adults will most be called to use is listening and speaking—on the job, in families, at the dry cleaners. The skills that will most impact their lives, though not the SAT, are skills that are least developed at school in a deliberate, substantive, assessed way!

Socratic seminar helps students hone these skills, as they clarify positions and learn the language of civil disagreement. Do we not have an obligation to teach these skills, essential for our democracy; to tolerate opposing viewpoints rather than attacking, to defend a point of view with evidence and logic rather than with anger and put-downs? Socrates was forced to drink hemlock for promoting this kind of thinking!

Likewise, seminar is not communication for the sheer enjoyment of the pursuit of knowledge, as Socrates' lofty motivations would suggest. In our real world of school, what is graded is valued. Thus an entire chapter is devoted to assessment of seminar, a recognition of the reality that talk, like writing, must be evaluated, though not judged publicly during the seminar, if it is to be truly appreciated in the "system" we call *school*.

CONTROL

This final human need breathes in a dynamic way in seminar. Teachers control behavior tightly and the questions that are asked—when they are asked, how they are asked, to whom they are asked in the case of a followup, and if they are asked. They also control the wait time, the pauses to see if more responses are forthcoming. But they do not control the ideas—what is said, how it is said, or how long it takes to say it. When the balance of talk in middle and high school discussions approach 95% student talk and 5% teacher talk, this is one discussion for which students feel tremendous responsibility. A modicum of control over their school life and academic destiny is a tremendous benefit for students in seminar. They value the time and behave better, seeing the seminar as *their* time to be in control.

School people must create supportive environments that encourage students to risk sharing their thoughts about academic matters with each other. Students remember what their buddies say around the lunch table about a rap group, about a boyfriend, about last night's "Melrose Place." And through a seminar, they also remember what their buddies say about "I Have a Dream," *Cry, The Beloved Country*, or even an essay on quantum physics! As they hear each other's voices, they refine their own; they tend to stay focused, and they grow to appreciate each other's differences. These are typical academic and behavioral payoffs when seminars are incorporated.

BLOCK SCHEDULING AND SOCRATIC SEMINAR

Middle and high schools that are moving to longer blocks of instructional time often find that Socratic Seminar is a valuable strategy for both extending and expanding discussion to a 90-minute block and for tightening efficiency by saving all discussion of a novel or collection of readings on a topic to a single rich seminar episode.

In middle and high schools, the seminar strategy may be applied frequently, as much as once or twice a week in a 4/4 block schedule for English and social studies, where literature or primary documents are the texts for seminar. The strategy works beautifully for humanities courses that link these two subjects.

A 4/4 (semester/semester) block schedule with a double humanities block allows for up to a 3-hour seminar.

In a 4/4 block, the strategy may appear in an Anatomy and Physiology class a couple of times each 9 weeks or every other week in Earth Science where more topics have relevant links. In most other disciplines—for example science, mathematics, foreign languages, and vocational courses—Socratic Seminars offer an occasional strategy for teachers to use in making the content relevant and expandable.

On an A/B or alternating day schedule, seminar may occur as frequently as every other week in English, every third week in social studies, or once every 9 weeks or more as applicable in science, health or vocational classes. Math often establishes seminars occasionally both in the big picture of defining *infinity* and *empty set*, or examining the meaning of *line* or *point*. Students enjoy examining the writings of Aristotle, or they may read Euclid's "Geometry" or Asimov's "The Feeling of Power." Biology students may explore Rachel Carson's environmental treatise *Silent Spring* or an essay on genetic engineering. These readings are not used to "teach" mathematics equations or the DNA molecule but rather to generate thinking about the ideas and usefulness of math and the awesome capabilities and responsibilities of science.

Such meaning-making, placing the curriculum into context, and establishing emotional connection to content are all documented methods for locking in new learning (Sylvester, 1995). These are the catalysts for linking new learning with old, thus entering the new learning into the mental system. Add to this the freedom to explore, the absence of overt judgment, and the honoring of student divergent ideas, and you have what Thomas Armstrong calls a "cognitive greenhouse," the ingredients that he notes in *Awakening Genius in the Classroom*. Socratic Seminars tap this meaning-making frame in a powerful way and help motivate all types of students.

Unfortunately, much of middle and high school methodology—namely lecture, teacher-led Q&A, and individual pencil/paper/book tasks—inhibits sharing in a community, limits student communication about academic matters to monosyllables, and maintains tight teacher control that translates into silence. Many troubled kids just drop out. Gangs, not schools, massage their human and developmental needs. Other students accept that survival in school depends on complacency, conformity, and, above all, studied silence.

One thing is certain. These problems are all compounded when a block schedule traps students for longer than 55-minute classes in the absence of strategies, such as Socratic Seminars, that get teachers off the stage and students to center stage!

This book is a handbook for teachers with limited or no experience in facilitating a Socratic Seminar, particularly with a block schedule. Certainly there is more to it than sitting around a circle and asking a few bold questions. A key organizing principle is that students and teachers must understand their new roles, as well as the rules and responsibilities within their respective roles. Finding appropriate texts and writing strong questions often determine a seminar's potential for success. Another important task is designing pre- and postseminar activities and fitting the seminar into a broader lesson or unit design. Finally, the seminar, if it is to be embraced as a strategy, should be assessed, both as a student performance and as a teacher practice.

Figures 1.1 and 1.2 illustrate how the seminar plugs into a 4/4 block and an A/B alternating day schedule. An actual lesson and unit design for incorporating seminar into block appears in Chapter 7.

FIGURE 1.1. SOCRATIC SEMINAR IN 4/4 BLOCK: 90 MINUTES

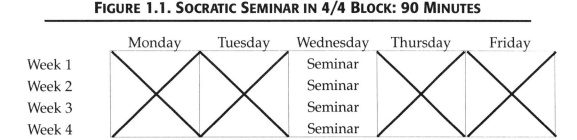

FIGURE 1.2. SOCRATIC SEMINAR IN A/B BLOCK: 90 MINUTES

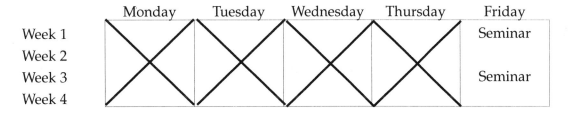

REFERENCES

Adler, M. J. (1982; 1984). *The Paideia Proposal*. New York: Macmillian.

Armstrong, T. (1998). *Awakening Genius in the Classroom*. Alexandria, VA: ASCD.

Dunn, R., and Dunn, K. (1992). *Teaching Secondary Student Through Their Individual Learning Syles*. Allyn & Bacon.

Kohn, K. (1993). *Punished by Rewards: The Trouble With Gold Stars, Incentive Plans, A's, Praise, and Other Bribes*. Boston: Houghton Mifflin.

Sylvester, R. (1995). *A Celebration of Neurons: An Educators Guide to the Human Brain*. Alexandria, VA: ASCD.

2

ROLES, RULES, AND RESPONSIBILITIES DURING A SEMINAR

"What is it you expect of me?" is the unspoken question every student either wants answered or needs answered on the first day of school. If he *wants* it answered, he is a convergent pleaser and derives comfort from the assurance of his teacher's specific expectations. He is assisted by seeing it in writing and gains confidence as he sees consistency in his teacher. If he *needs* it answered, he is a divergent dreamer who needs the harnessing of the teacher's specific expectation. He, too, is assisted by the reinforcement of seeing it in writing and retains focus as he sees consistency in his teacher.

Both students bring gifts to the seminar which enrich the experience. And both benefit from a clear understanding of how seminar is different from other classroom experiences, of what they must do and how they will respond, and of what function their teacher will have in all this.

Whether on a blocked schedule or not, it is a fairly singular experience for students to hear their teacher say:

> Today, after we ready this one-page essay aloud, and you complete your directed task on it (a preseminar activity), we are going to form a circle. I'll ask a few questions, but it's your seminar. *I can't say anything about the reading*. But I know you will figure it out! Oh, and it should last 30 minutes or so.

Students glance at each other with that, "Has she lost her mind?" look or return a puzzled, and often skeptical, eye back to the teacher. "'It's *your* seminar—*you* will figure it out.' And the teacher cannot talk? What is going on here?" The dawning for students is that this will be no ordinary class discussion. Consider this too typical scenario for "class discussion":

> Teacher asks a question. No one answers. Teacher asks again, maybe adding a hint. One student answers. Teacher asks for other opinions. None are forthcoming. Teacher fills in with opinions. Teacher asks

another question. Student answers. Teacher asks if anyone can add to this. One student does, briefly. Teacher follows with lengthy explanation....

Admittedly, a class discussion is not always this bad, but too often the role of the teacher is that of rescuer. Students know that if they do not speak, the teacher will fill in the gaps and tell them what they need to know. This enabling teacher behavior reinforces student apathy. Why should students participate if the teacher will do all the work? It becomes a kind of passive game. Teachers ask questions, and students have responses in their heads but often only access them if called on.

Or, worse, they pass with "I don't know" to avoid the possible ridicule of, "Can someone *add to* Mary's answer?" The teacher was just trying to extend the thinking to other students, but the inherent judgment of the child's shortcoming in needing her answer "added to" is enough to cause this child and likely others never to speak in a class discussion, even when they have an answer or an opinion. It is a revelation for teachers to think that in their efforts to get a discussion going, they are crippling the thinking that would do just that each time they judge, add to, fill in, or further explain after they call for a student answer or opinion. Too often the discussion dies for lack of a second and turns into a lecture with sporadic questions and mini-answers from students. Teachers will report that it is difficult or even impossible to get a class to discuss anything. "They just do not seem to care; they have no opinions!" are the teachers' resigned conclusions as they throw in the towel and return to the dog-eared notes.

The seminar setting will change this dynamic by design, both with ground rules for discussion of texts and with roles and procedures that ensure student interest and ownership. A good class discussion feels much like a seminar when dialogue starts to flow and students engage each other; however, a regular class discussion achieves a high level of active engagement more by chance than by design. When students know the teacher is out of the discussion and won't agree or disagree, they rise to the occasion, carry on the dialogue, and, most importantly, prepare the assignment. In the seminar, there is nowhere to hide! Figure 2.1 lists differences between a seminar and a typical question-answer class discussion.

Two obvious distinctions between a Socratic Seminar and a usual class discussion are ownership and feedback. Ownership appears clearly in the hands of students though teachers adjust the sails. It is the power of asking profound questions that the teacher holds. Once the question, which fishes broadly, is asked, the teacher's real "power to empower" is *silence*. The transfer of ownership for talk now resides with students to examine the ideas and issues of text.

It is always fascinating to see that when a student offers the first response in seminar, all participants look back to the teacher, like lemmings to the sea, waiting for reaction. Was the student right, wrong, half wrong ("Can anyone help John

---

FIGURE 2.1. DIFFERENCES BETWEEN SOCRATIC SEMINAR AND CLASS DISCUSSION

Socratic Seminars	Class Discussions
Students and teacher are in a circle. All have eye contact; teacher is on the same level.	Students are often in rows. Teacher is set apart and often higher on a stool or behind a podium.
97% student talk; students know teacher won't comment.	97% teacher talk, even if many questions are asked. Teacher elaborates and answers.
Average response for students is 8–12 seconds.	Average response for students is 2–3 seconds.
No verbal or nonverbal approval is present. Affirming feedback by the teacher is taboo.	Teacher affirmation of correctness is typical. Sustaining feedback for incorrectness is expected.
Thinking, backed up with textual evidence, is paramount. Open-ended exploration, not rightness, is valued.	Rightness is usually paramount; thinking ends as soon as someone is right.
Students listen primarily to peers.	Students listen primarily to the teacher, who has the answer.
Students have ownership for most of the flow.	Teachers have ownership for most of the flow.
Students are held accountable for contributions based upon criteria that have been agreed upon.	Students see discussion as a frill, a nebulous, negligible "participation grade." If you miss class, you didn't miss much.

---

out...?") or half right ("An interesting point but...")? When there is no visible reaction and certainly no comments from the teacher, students soon abandon the training of years of teacher judgment and sink into their thinking.

Certainly it is clear from studies on thinking that the thinking act occurs with greater frequency and depth in the absence of risk, judgment, or fear. (Armstrong, 1998; Kohn, 1993). Imagine the invitation to think in a class discussion where all outward signs of these barriers are removed, both from teachers and from classmates. The result, if teacher controlled conditions are met, is consistently rich and energetic levels of student talk about content.

SNAPSHOT OF A SOCRATIC SEMINAR

So what does a Socratic seminar look like? The following is a vertical view of a seminar, from beginning to end:

♦ Students arrive for the seminar, taking their places in a circle with the teacher. If the seminar text (an essay, poem, novel, primary document, artwork, etc.) has been assigned, they arrive with their text marked and with notes and page references.

♦ The teacher asks an open-ended "opening question" to send the students into the text and then waits in silence.

♦ Now students respond, after teacher acknowledgment, to express a view, to cite evidence, and to examine, support, and disagree with the ideas of others. They look at each other, not at the teacher, unless they are seeking acknowledgment to speak.

♦ The teacher takes notes for evaluative purposes but provides no verbal or nonverbal feedback that either affirms or challenges what the students say. The teacher may ask follow-up questions for clarification, or probing questions to push student thinking that is shallow or erroneous; however, questions are used sparingly and deliberately. The teacher is off this stage.

♦ When satisfied that the opening question has been thoroughly explored, the seminar leader asks one or more "core questions" to examine central points of the text.

♦ Students know this is their seminar. The teacher will ask the question, after which students direct most of the seminar. It is not uncommon for 15–20 student responses to arise from a single good Socratic question, or for the exploration of one question to last from 30–60 minutes.

♦ Once the text has been explored thoroughly (or time is running short) the teacher asks a "closing question," which springs from the text but which seeks to have students connect some issue from the text with their lives. At this stage, personal anecdotes may be shared, vulnerabilities may be exposed, real emotion may be expressed. This question is the one that often locks some ideas from the text to the students' long-term memories. Time and again, young people remember some idea about a particular text several years later because they recall something powerful a classmate said or something that was poignantly revealed in seminar.

♦ The seminar is over when it's over. For one class, 5–10 prepared questions may take 45 minutes, with the teacher asking all 10 questions. Another class may talk for 60 minutes on the opening question. Seminars take on a life of their own because they are steered largely by students, with the teacher's occasional course corrections through questioning.

STUDENT RESPONSIBILITIES AND RULES DURING SEMINAR

Students are better prepared for seminar when they have been taught their responsibilities and are held accountable for them. Figure 2.2. is a declaration of student responsibilities in a Socratic Seminar.

FIGURE 2.2. DECLARATION OF STUDENT RESPONSIBILITIES IN SOCRATIC SEMINAR

Thinking: I am responsible for...

- ◆ Pausing and thinking before I respond to the facilitator's question or to a comment made by a peer.
- ◆ Locating facts and examples in the text that can be cited as evidence for a particular argument.
- ◆ Searching for connections with previous readings or prior studies.
- ◆ Being willing to change my opinion if more information is given or if my reasoning has been flawed.
- ◆ Seeing the relevance of the reading to my world.
- ◆ Being prepared by having read my text thoroughly and reflectively.
- ◆ Having marked key issues in my text.

Speaking: I am responsible for...

- ◆ Asking questions about what I have read, heard, and seen.
- ◆ Asking for clarification of any passage I have read but which I do not understand.
- ◆ Giving my opinions clearly yet succinctly.
- ◆ Making judgments that I can defend with textual evidence.
- ◆ Focusing on the question at hand.
- ◆ Explaining to others how I have inferred an idea by exploring the passage that has led me to this conclusion.
- ◆ Disagreeing with the ideas of others, not with the people.
- ◆ Clarifying information and lending support to a peer's argument.
- ◆ Taking issue with inaccuracies or illogical reasoning.
- ◆ Moving the seminar forward to new concepts.
- ◆ Returning the seminar to a previous topic if new insights arise.
- ◆ Speaking loudly and articulating clearly.
- ◆ Directing comments to peers, not to the teacher.

Listening: I am responsible for…

♦ Listening attentively and patiently as peers share their ideas.

♦ Listening critically to others' opinions so that I may take issue with inaccuracies or illogical reasoning.

♦ Maintaining an open mind to a diversity of opinions.

♦ Listening acutely to a peer's entire position before taking issue with it.

♦ Avoiding repetitiveness by developing stronger listening skills.

Self-Awareness: I am responsible for…

♦ Raising my hand and getting teacher acknowledgment before speaking.

♦ Exercising patience and self control.

♦ Being courteous and respectful of my peers.

♦ Avoiding all side conversations.

♦ Avoiding body language with negative connotations.

THINKING DURING SEMINAR

For thinking, teachers may emphasize the importance of thinking before speaking. This usually poses no problem for the introverted thinker, who processes internally anyway, listens to others and continues processing. This student may never feel "moved" to speak without some encouragement. He may prove to be the student who, like E. F. Hutton, speaks briefly at the end of the seminar, nailing the most succinct, potent observation that blows the class away. The admonition to "think before speaking" really addresses the extroverted thinker who often figures out what he is thinking as he says it out loud. Forcing this student to think first deliberately and form the completed thought, even writing it down first, will help to harness the talk, keeping it organized and tight. A challenge for this student is not to ramble and cause others to lose interest. Therefore, training students to be aware of their cognitive habits is important. They are urged to think about their thinking.

The declaration also addresses thinking in three additional areas: preparation for the seminar; search for textual evidence and inference; and recognition of relevance and connection of the text to the student's experience. A student was overheard as he left his first seminar, in which he uttered not a word, saying, "Gee, I've never had to think so hard in my life!" The talk, in other words, gave no indication of this child's inner dialogue, which was rich and is one reason that talk alone does not determine a child's grade in seminar.

Speaking During Seminar

Speaking is, however, a goal. For if a class full of reflective, introverted thinkers held a seminar, they may sit there considering for an hour with no one feeling moved to speak. Even in a 90-minute block, time is precious. There is no seminar without talk. Students should know up front that not to speak requires them to submit an alternate assignment tomorrow. Teachers are simply focusing students on some basic rules for discourse, namely that they follow their views with evidence, citing from their text with a paraphrase or quote. They are urged to hold an opinion, clarify a point, make a judgment, even to disagree or lend support. These goals are accomplished with textual proof or inferences and through language that is clear and free from attack.

Furthermore, speaking is encouraged to raise questions, ask for clarification, or return to a subject that further reflection has sparked. Worthy speaking refocuses the group on the question at hand or moves to new issues. Students feel liberated in this role, seeking the teacher's eye only for permission to speak and feeling keenly responsible for what is happening in the class.

Listening During Seminar

A third area of student responsibility is the development of strong listening skills. Often the students with the biggest and most frequent voices are the weakest listeners. "Listen twice, speak once" is good advice for them. In seminar it becomes quite obvious if some students aren't listening carefully. They begin to repeat what someone else has said or disagree with a statement that was not made. Or they let pass an inaccuracy or try to cut someone off before her point is made.

A real challenge for students is not to block listening when they disagree with what someone says. For only by listening carefully can they refute and cite text to take issue with a point of view and accurately reflect their specific opposition. Hearing someone out is a key life skill at work and in personal relationships. In seminar, it is taught, acknowledged, and rewarded!

Self-Awareness During Seminar

The seminar establishes a setting where all must feel free to express their ideas without reprisal. Put-downs—through words, gestures, or even looks—are taboo. Good teachers do not tolerate personal insults among students anyway, but on seminar day, this rule must carry a heightened awareness. Even good-natured, gentle teasing is out. Students are taught to disagree with someone's ideas, not with the person. Much as the lobster goes to the bottom of the sea to a recessed and protected area to shed its old exoskeleton and secrete a new one, students must be in a "safe" environment to expose their thoughtful vulnerabilities in an hour or two of dialogue. All it takes is one student's tolerated rudeness to another to shut down some in the seminar for the rest of the year. The risk is too great for them.

Another rule addresses general courtesy and self-control. Waiting one's turn, choosing disagreement language carefully, staying focused, and thinking before speaking are all expected of seminar participants.

A potentially innocuous act like two students having a brief side conversation can have a devastating effect on seminar. Other than the sheer rudeness of two people talking while someone else has the floor, the speaker may think the aside is about her and view it as criticism. Or the talk may not bother the speaker at all but have a stifling effect on another student who may never speak for fear of being talked about.

Of all the responsibilities of students in seminar, the most important are the self-awareness issues. There is no seminar if students do not feel safe, so these are emphasized for every seminar, as is the speaking responsibility related to disagreeing amicably with ideas, not with people.

It would be useful to share a short list of seminar rules, with a heavy focus on self awareness, for students going into their first seminars. The "Declaration of Student Responsibilities" may be too much to keep in mind as students first begin to learn the seminar process. Figure 2.3 shows initial seminar rules with student self-assessment.

FIGURE 2.3. INITIAL SOCRATIC SEMINAR RULES

Initial Socratic Seminar Rules	*Fully*	*Partially*	*Not Yet*
		Accomplished	
Raised hand, got acknowledgment to speak			
Was courteous and respectful to peers			
Exercised patience and self control			
Disagreed with ideas, not people			
Listened carefully to peers			
Participated verbally			
Thought before spoke			
Supported opinions with text where possible			

Name: _____

Seminar on: _____

These "Initial Socratic Seminar Rules" are all that are needed. Students keep their list before them during seminar and monitor their success in following the rules. As they gain facility, they become responsible for all items in the Declaration. Eventually, they will be graded on their contributions using the rubric in the assessment chapter.

The bottom-line for seminar rules is that they must be thoroughly understood and consistently enforced. Most students will do what their teachers expect if these two factors are present. Appropriate behaviors must be specifically taught and modeled; inappropriate behaviors must be swiftly, gently, but always, corrected.

SEMINARS WITH AT-RISK STUDENTS

Some teachers report apprehension at using seminar in some classes that include particularly troubled and troublesome youngsters. However, our experience has been that at-risk students particularly enjoy this process so much that they behave for the seminar while they may present challenges on other days. They likewise will prepare their assignment for seminar, but often do not complete other types of homework. It seems that the chance to be heard and to hear their peers is incentive enough for some students, once hooked on the strategy, to modify their behaviors and complete often challenging assignments.

However, a teacher who has difficulty managing student behavior anyway may have trouble managing it in seminar. If this is the case, the seminar should be abandoned if students don't "come around." If their safety cannot be guaranteed, the strategy is useless and other methods, less dependent on behaviors linked to trust and freedom, must be sought.

A final note about "at-risk" students regards the often bright child who no longer speaks in class because of the fear of peers. Who wants to be labeled "teacher's pet" or "brown nose" for answering questions? "What are you trying to prove?" or "Who are you trying to impress?" become the not-so-subtle messages of icy looks to students who would break the code of cool and participate in a discussion. "At risk" has many faces, and this one may exist in epidemic proportion in honors, college track, or AP programs where student judgments of each other are lethal. The safety rules and intrigue of seminar may be just the antidote for this spreading cancer.

TEACHER RESPONSIBILITIES AND RULES DURING SEMINAR

Teachers often look and behave differently in seminar than in any other teaching setting. And students should be apprised of this change. Otherwise, they may misread their teacher's intentions. Just as students must adhere to a responsibility code, teachers also have a code. Figure 2.4 lists teacher responsibilities in most of the same areas as students.

Figure 2.4. Teacher Behaviors During Seminar

Self-Awareness

- Seat at same level as students
- Eye contact possible with every child
- No eye contact with speaker after acknowledgment to speak
- Room scanned for behaviors, hands up, eye contact with those on verge of hand up
- Neutral facial expressions—no agreement/disagreement
- Low affect—minimal body language, point to speakers

Speaking

- Use clear and measured tone—not loud
- Ask questions in order by type
- Give students "credit" for ideas in questions where possible
- Call for clarification with followups
- Stop inappropriate behaviors every time
- Do not express a view or opinion

Listening

- For repetitions to occur
- For insights to be made
- For new ideas to emerge
- For core issues to be raised
- For generalizations to question
- For exhaustion of a point
- For silence—generous wait time for thinking

Writing

- To chart student response
- To record codes for student responses
- To note new points
- To mark off key ideas and issues that are covered
- To mark off questions that have been explored
- To record phrases that will be turned into core questions
- To cite students for credit on core questions

The teacher's role in seminar shifts to listener, facilitator, enabler, clarifier, manager, and judge. The first five roles are overt, observable behaviors that direct the broad flow and some of the specifics of the discussion. All questioning and teacher comment should stimulate thoughtful discussion, draw out issues, request reasons or justification in the text, rephrase questions, or paraphrase answers for increased clarity. The teacher may begin, "Are you saying that...?" and summarize his or her understanding of a student's two-minute ramble. Such questions ask for clarification and may push circular thinkers to collapse their thoughts into succinct points. Asking, "Where in the text do you find evidence for that?" prevents a student from making a point just to hear the sound of his or her own voice. Followup questions that call for evidence ensure that the text is thoroughly explored, not just dusted in generalities. This is no bull session or lovefest where all answers are equally appropriate and worthy. Like Socrates, the teacher's role is to push the thinking without giving students ideas or *appearing* to judge.

The "manager" function is met as the teacher enforces the rules, though the ultimate goal is for students to manage their own behaviors. There are times, however, when even well-trained seminar participants react to highly charged issues. The seminar leader must step in and uphold the rules about waiting for acknowledgment, thinking before speaking, and disagreeing with ideas, not people. If the need arises to correct behaviors, the teacher should say, "Let's leave the seminar for a moment while I address an infraction of the rules." It is important to "leave" the seminar because the teacher's voice must take the floor for something other than questioning.

The toughest job of the seminar leader is to listen actively, take good notes, judge the responses of all speakers, but never engage in the dialogue to express an opinion. Teachers report sitting on their hands, biting their lips, and keeping their eyes down to avoid getting personally involved. Students are accustomed to answering a question in a class discussion and then looking to the teacher for validation or correction. Usually they can count on us for both! But any thinking about the question by students often ends as the teacher responds.

Seminar leaders must focus their energy on tracking and judging student comments and remembering that as long as teachers are not talking, students are still thinking and speaking! Seminar leaders must never agree or disagree, nod approval or look askance. All judgments are in the teachers' notes during seminar, not on their faces or in their voices.

For some, the "poker face" can prevail. Others find that their outgoing and nurturing personalities have difficulty with this part. These teachers might practice a pleasant "studied nod" that says, "Thank you for contributing; I understand what you are saying, but I'm not giving you any feedback about the quality of what you are saying."

Of course, after seminar, teachers are free to praise, wink, hug, or otherwise engage individual students. It just cannot be done during the seminar, when the goal is for participants to explore the text thoroughly for understanding. Outward teacher judgment would interfere, changing the dynamic to teacher as keeper of the truth. Corrections and issues that should have arisen but did not, or ideas that were not explored fully, may all be placed in tonight's assignment or on tomorrow's lesson plan!

To outward observers, teachers do not appear to be doing much during the seminar. Observers mistake the teacher's deliberately low- key role as passive and relaxed. However, teachers report that seminars are exhausting. They simultaneously scan, chart responses, make notes, and listen for generalizations or connections to other speakers and to core questions. It is challenging for teachers to lead two seminars back-to-back, given the heightened listening and other tasks. As one seasoned seminar teacher noted, "It's the most exhausting class period you will ever *not* teach!"

REFERENCES

Armstrong, T. (1998). *Awakening Genius in the Classroom.* Alexandria, VA: ASCD.

Kohn, K. (1993). *Punished by Rewards: The Trouble With Gold Stars, Incentive Plans, A's, Praise, and Other Bribes.* Boston: Houghton Mifflin.

3

PREPARING THE CLASSROOM AND READER FOR SOCRATIC SEMINARS

PREPARING THE CLASSROOM FOR SOCRATIC SEMINARS

Cooperative teams, learning centers, Socratic Seminars—all of these teaching strategies require some temporary rearrangement of the classroom. For seminar, all students must be seated in a circle where there is eye contact among them. Because students converse with each other, not just with the teacher, both students and the seminar leader should be seated on the same level within the circle. While facilitating the seminar, the teacher wants to blend into the group and not be perceived as an authority figure, which can best be achieved by the circle design. To have better visibility for monitoring, a teacher may be tempted to sit on a stool above the group. This is not a good idea because it makes the teacher the focus of attention. In seminar, teachers and students are on the same level of seating which equalizes their importance in the seminar. In a great seminar, students become so engrossed in the issues that they forget the teacher is even there. For teachers and students alike, the seminar is a euphoric experience when students are engaged in animated intellectual discourse.

"How do I arrange my classroom for seminar?" "What can I do when I have too many students for the circle?" "How can I incorporate seminar when I teach in a science lab with fixed tables?" These are questions many teachers ask as they experience seminar for the first time. They have no doubt the process works, but logistical concerns for implementation are very real. Unfortunately, there are no easy answers, for every school has its own unique problems with space demands and class size. Finding ways to overcome these barriers, however, is worth the effort, even if it means switching rooms with another teacher for the period or bringing in folding chairs. Because the seminar is not a strategy that is used daily, the inconvenience of room rearrangement is manageable for most teachers.

21

Although classroom sizes vary, most rooms can accommodate a circle of 25–30 student desks; however, a circle of more than 30 may present some problems. In this case the inner/outer circle, which is discussed later in the chapter, may be used so that a circle can be formed. For students to talk to each other, they must have the eye contact afforded by the seminar circle. Communication is most effective when participants are speaking and listening directly to each other with all physical barriers removed.

In forming the seminar circle, student desks are more desirable than single chairs such as folding chairs. First of all, desks allow students to manipulate their text and take notes more easily than if when they are holding the text on their laps. Additionally, desks give more personal space to each student and eliminate potential distractions caused by close proximity. Regardless of the type of seating the teacher must use, a circle is crucial for "equalizing" students. In a circle, no student is thrust into a prominent position at the front, nor is a student able to hide away in a corner. Instead, each is invited to become an integral part of the seminar process.

What is an appropriate size for seminar? What happens when class numbers exceed the recommended size or when the classroom itself is tiny? First, ideal class size for seminar is 25 or fewer students; however, most teachers have at least one class that exceeds the ideal. For these larger groups, variations must be made in the circle setup. When class size is over 30, the physical environment may be cramped and uncomfortable. More significantly, in larger classes students are limited in seminar participation opportunities.

INNER/OUTER CIRCLES

To alleviate these problems—and to create special opportunities—teachers use an inner/outer circle arrangement, which consists of two layers of seating with the second layer in a horseshoe design facing the facilitator. The horseshoe design prevents students from sitting outside the teacher's range of vision. A full outer circle is impossible to monitor effectively because there is no visibility when students are seated behind the teacher.

While inner circle participants are the primary speakers in seminar, the outer circle students are not excluded. Within the inner circle, empty chairs, called "hot seats," are placed strategically on all three sides to enable outer circle students to participate in the discussion. As they desire to speak, students quietly leave the outer row and move into a "hot seat" where they are recognized as fully functioning members of the inner circle. Once they have been acknowledged, however, they vacate the "hot seat" and move back to their original position on the outer circle, thus making the "hot seat" available for the next student to come from the outer circle.

FIGURE 3.1. INNER/OUTER CIRCLE DIAGRAM

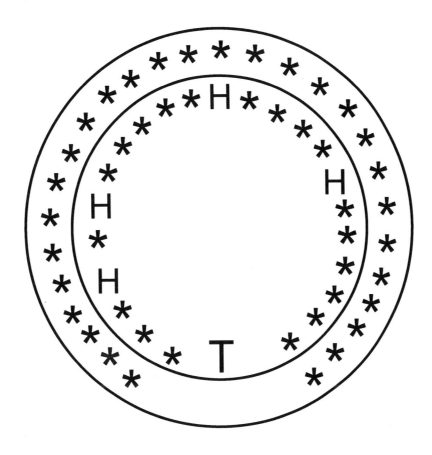

T = Teacher's Seat
* = Students
H = Hot seats

OUTER CIRCLE CONSIDERATIONS

Although teachers find it necessary to use the inner/outer construction, this arrangement should be occasional. Students generally dislike the format, feeling excluded or punished. Even with the accessibility of "hot seats," students on the outer circle do not have the same level of participation as the inner circle. Understandably, there is frustration for the talkative students; however, they respond positively if the inner/outer circle is not a weekly experience, and the teacher's reason for using the design is apparent.

Outer circle members should always be assigned a specific task in addition to observing the seminar. Unless students have an assignment that focuses their listening skills, the outer circle will not work effectively, and these students may tune out or become disruptive. First of all, teachers should use the inner/outer arrangement only when necessary and for deliberate teaching objectives. For example, an English instructor, in an effort to evaluate and give speedier feedback, may elect to have half the class write compositions one week and the other half write their essays the following week. With this as the goal, outer circle participants use the seminar by brainstorming and taking notes for their compositions, and include their notes as prewriting in the processed writing evaluation. After having heard the text explored in seminar, no student should complain of having "nothing to write" or lack depth in his writing when issues have been raised, and textual references have been cited. During the next week, another seminar text is discussed, and the process is reversed. Each student has been a member of both the inner and outer circles and has produced a processed writing based on a seminar text.

While outer circle tasks are as varied as the teacher's imagination, these tasks should link directly with curricular objectives. Tasks should never be busywork, but should be meaningful learning experiences. Outer circle tasks are usually assessed as part of a followup assignment that only outer circle participants do, and placement on the outer circle is made to specifically achieve this goal. While some teachers prefer assessing outer circle performance as an independent activity, most teachers assign a grade to the outer circle task as part of a larger assignment. For instance, if all students, both inner and outer circle, are completing a post seminar writing, likely the notes taken by the outer circle are graded as prewriting, not as an entirely separate grade. There are no absolutes on grading of outer circle tasks. The task itself should define the grading method and points assigned to outer circle tasks.

Occasionally, outer circle participants may be asked to assess the conversation within the inner circle; however, in most classes this occurs infrequently. While peer assessment is helpful in reminding students of desired seminar behaviors, it is not needed after every seminar. For the most part, outer circle members need to be engaged in activities that increase their own learning. Figure 3.2 suggests five outer circle tasks that effectively engage students in the seminar.

BENEFITS OF THE INNER/OUTER CIRCLE FORMAT

Are there added benefits of the inner/outer format? Absolutely! Use of the inner/outer circle format facilitates combining classes for team-teaching experiences or grouping of students within the classroom. For instance, bringing American literature and United States history students together is a logical teaching approach that can prevent repetition of the curriculum; many teachers, however, fail to do so because they have no method of combining 50 or more students in an organized, orderly manner. When teachers use the inner/outer circle to combine classes for integrated English and history seminars, there is controlled movement and structured activity. Under these circumstances, the joining of classes is not only feasible but also desirable.

FIGURE 3.2. SUGGESTED OUTER CIRCLE TASKS

- ◆ Peer-evaluate one or more inner circle participants using a checklist of observable behaviors. (See Chapter 9, "Assessment of Seminars.")

- ◆ Take notes as brainstorming and prewriting for an essay.

- ◆ List significant themes or issues discussed in the seminar. (Teacher asks an outer circle student to close the seminar by recapping the main points covered in seminar. This focuses students on astute listening.)

- ◆ Record issues or themes which arose in the seminar but were not adequately explored or were not documented. Require students to elaborate on these points or to find documentation to share with the class following seminar.

- ◆ After the seminar ends, outer circle members form a think/pair/share with someone from the inner circle. Here, they share views on particular issues discussed in the seminar. Peer-evaluation feedback can also be given at this time.

Another benefit of inner/outer circle is the emphasis it places on preparation for seminar. Reading readiness is a must in student preparation, so this is emphasized. Unfortunately, many students still come unprepared to class; consequently, teachers may require their students to qualify for seminar by taking an objective reading quiz or by completing some other preseminar reading evaluation. Those students who do not meet the instructor's reading standards may be relegated to the outer circle. At first, this placement process appears purely punitive, but it actually serves several purposes. It sorts students into two sections—the prepared and the less prepared. If a core group has not adequately read the material, the seminar is doomed, so the teacher needs this information before proceeding. The attention given to reading readiness encourages students to be prepared. Finally, placing students on the outer circle gives less proficient readers a chance to use the portion of reading they have completed successfully. By going to the "hot seat," they can still contribute substantially to the seminar. Along with any verbal contributions from the "hot seat," outer circle participants have their assigned tasks and must complete their reading. Hopefully, the richness of seminar has made that reading more interesting and rewarding.

Teachers also find the inner/outer circle arrangement useful when a longer seminar text has been assigned. Longer texts generally equate to longer seminars which, depending on the makeup of the class, may pose some attention problems. For example, students with attention deficit disorders have greater difficulty attending in a longer stretch of time without a break. To insure success for these students, use of inner/outer circle lets the teacher switch participants somewhere in the middle of the seminar. On a 90-minute block, 45 minutes for each group to be on the inner circle is possible. Switching the inner/ outer participants focuses each group specifically on either speaking or listening skills, both of which are equally valuable. Figure 3.3 is an overview of the inner/outer circle concept.

FIGURE 3.3. OVERVIEW OF INNER/OUTER CIRCLE

- What is "inner/outer circle"?

  This is a way of arranging the room for seminar with two layers of seating with several chairs on the outer circle labeled as "hot seats." Students seated within the inner circle are participants in seminar; those seated in the outer circle are observers.

- Under what conditions should I use inner/outer circle?
  - When I have students who qualify for the seminar.
  - When I have an extra large class.
  - When two classes are combined.
  - When I have a specific teaching objective.

- What are "hot seats"?

  Hot seats allow students on the outer circle to participate as a member of the inner circle. When the student moves to the hot seat, he can be recognized to speak. Upon making his comment, he must vacate the hot seat and return to his outer circle chair and resume any duties he has been assigned as an outer circle member.

- Is it fair to exclude students from the seminar?

  Use of this design does not exclude students when the hot seats are available. As long as students have opportunities to be part of both circles, the fairness is maintained.

- How do I maintain control over the outer circle while I am leading the seminar?

  Outer circle members must have a clearly defined task as well as rules and expectations that are firmly enforced.

- How frequently should I use this concept?

  Use it sparingly and with purpose. Don't have the same people repeatedly on the outer circle.

PREPARING THE READER FOR SEMINAR

For what reason will a seminar always fail? It will fail for the class when the majority of students have not adequately read and will fail for individual students who have shortchanged themselves on reading. One of the most important components in seminar is preparing the reader.

One might ask, "What is the big deal? Students are asked to read for every class." When most students read a selection, they read with the goal of passing an objective quiz or of playing a minor role in a class discussion. Primarily, they are reading for facts only, paying little attention to issues and implications. In most anthologies, the questions at the end of selections are arranged beginning with facts, moving to interpretation, and finally ending with implications. Often the largest section deals with facts. Early experience has taught students that the quiz likely comes from section one—the facts—because interpretation and implications are harder to score. Their energy in reading, consequently, is devoted to factual recall.

No one is denying the significance of knowing the facts, but seminar reading readiness must go beyond the obvious. In a sense, teachers, in instructing their class in the seminar strategy, must retrain their students about how to read a text. Additionally, into every lesson teachers must build strategies to insure that the reading is getting done.

First, students need instruction on how to read a seminar text and explanation as to how this reading is different from their normal reading. A good place to begin is with a discussion of critical reading. Reading critically involves organizing information, thinking analytically, and going beyond facts into ideas and meaning. Reading for seminar requires reading for total understanding of facts and concepts. A cursory reading to glean facts is not adequate preparation for seminar. Students must probe deeply into key concepts, issues, and implications. Unless students make sense of what they have read, they will have nothing of significance to contribute to the seminar. In *How to Read a Book,* Adler and Van Doren (1972) describe three stages in analytical reading that are useful to discuss with students (Figure 3.4).

DIRECTED READING FOR SEMINAR

Directed reading activities (which may or may not be the preseminar assignment) are excellent ways to guide students in critical reading. As well, teachers may use the same questions to guide their own reading before preparing seminar questions. A seminar facilitator must be an astute critical reader who is a step ahead of the students in order to anticipate the direction the seminar may progress. Leading a seminar is a mental workout for every teacher, so reading preparation must be intense.

To increase reading comprehension and readiness for seminar, students must learn concrete strategies to improve their overall reading. Five methods are presented for consideration—directed reading activity models; three-level study guides; tips for marking a text; graphic organization; and student reading guides.

FIGURE 3.4. THE THREE STAGES OF ANALYTICAL READING

- ◆ The First Stage of Analytical Reading
  - Classify the book according to kind and subject matter.
  - State what the whole book is about with utmost brevity.
  - Enumerate its major parts in their order and relation, and outline these parts as you have outlined the whole.
  - Define the problem or problems the author has tried to solve.
- ◆ The Second Stage of Analytical Reading: Rules for Interpreting a Book's Contents
  - Come to terms with the author by interpreting his key words.
  - Grasp the author's leading propositions by dealing with his most important sentences.
  - Know the author's arguments, by finding them in, or constructing them out of, sequences of sentences.
  - Determine which of his problems the author has solved, and which he has not; and on the latter, decide which the author knew he had failed to solve.
- ◆ The Third Stage of Analytical Reading: Rules for Criticizing a Book as a Communication of Knowledge
  - General Maxims of Intellectual Etiquette
    - Do not begin criticism until you have completed your outline and your interpretation of the book. Do not say you agree, disagree, or suspend judgment, until you can say, "I understand."
    - Do not disagree disputatiously or contentiously.
    - Demonstrate that you recognize the difference between knowledge and mere personal opinion by presenting good reasons for any critical judgment you make.
  - Special Criteria for Points of Criticism
    - Show wherein the author is uninformed.
    - Show wherein the author is misinformed.
    - Show wherein the author is illogical.
    - Show wherein the author's analysis or account is incomplete.

    Note: Of these last four, the first three are criteria for disagreement. Failing in all of these, you must agree, at least in part, although you may suspend judgment on the whole, in light to the last point.

DIRECTED READING ACTIVITY MODEL

A directed reading is not the same as study questions from a novel. While study questions may serve a purpose in a longer work, too frequently students view them as "busywork." If these questions must be used, fewer broad questions are preferable to many specific questions. An effective directed reading task for seminar is limited to 10 questions that cause the student to organize, analyze, and think critically about the text.

The directed reading activities included in Figures 3.5, 3.6 (p. 30), and 3.7 (p. 32) are useful tools in seminar preparation. All three activities can be adapted for use with a variety of seminar texts. Activity 1 requires students to make key inferences about the text before discussing it in seminar. This advance thinking primes them for the opening question and encourages deeper analysis of the text.

FIGURE 3.5. SEMINAR DIRECTED READING: ACTIVITY 1

1. What type of reading is this text, and what is the author's purpose for writing?

2. Briefly, what is the selection about?

3. What main points does the author make?

4. What problem(s) has the author tried to solve?

5. List five key words and phrases. What do these mean?

6. With what in the text do you agree? Disagree?

7. List five quotes and draw an inference from each one.

8. Describe three characters in three or fewer words. Give an action of the character's that illustrates your description.

9. How does the selection end? Are the conflicts resolved?

10. From this reading, what is relevant to my life and to society?

In high school English and middle school Language Arts classes, short stories and novels are frequently text for seminar. Every teacher wants to promote better reading comprehension and appreciation for good literature; however, most teachers want something more—for students to connect the literature to their own world in order to gain some insight into human nature. By giving students an opportunity to discuss the literature in seminar, all these goals can be accomplished. Yes, students need to understand theme, plot, and irony, but these terms do not have to be taught by the seminar. Activity 2 requires students to analyze plot, theme, mood, and character motivations. During the seminar the teacher will see what concepts students have gleaned from their reading. Afterwards, out of the seminar format, they can use the activity sheet for detailed review of the selection. Although it's tempting to want every item to be covered in seminar, teachers must refrain from controlling the seminar too tightly. There is always time for teacher input after students' discussion ends.

FIGURE 3.6. SEMINAR DIRECTED READING: ACTIVITY 2

1. Summarize the plot of the story in a page or less.

2. Diagram the plot outline:
   - ◆ Exposition:
     - • Setting
     - • Characters
   - ◆ Rising action:
     - • Conflict
     - • Motivations
     - • Dramatic climax
   - ◆ Climax

   - ◆ Resolution

3. List the major character(s) and analyze physical/personality traits and motivations for behavior.

4. Identify the theme, mood, and point of view.

5. What are the outcomes of major conflicts?

Often when students read a text, especially a novel, they complain that they don't really know what is important and what isn't. Activity 3 focuses student attention on specific items. As they locate references in the text, they start drawing inferences about what these items mean and how these are interrelated throughout the reading. The first time students discuss a novel, they really benefit from this specificity. Hopefully, their preparation skills will develop sufficiently where they can mark their text without as much direction. With lower reading levels or with younger students, Activity 3 may be used more frequently until marking skills are strengthened.

THREE-LEVEL STUDY GUIDES

Another way to assist students in reading for seminar is through teacher-made three-level study guides. Three-level study guides are one component of Richardson and Morgan's *Reading to Learn in the Content Areas*. Three-level guides work equally well for fiction and nonfiction. While these guides are not as lengthy as traditional study guides, they effectively determine accuracy of reading for facts, inferences, and application. Before beginning three-level guides, students should read the text, then use the text to complete the guide. These should never be used as quizzes with texts closed, which altogether defeats the purpose for using the three-level guides. Because each guide has approximately 15 questions, encourage students to write correct responses or comments about why the answer given is illogical. Initially, significant preparation time is needed to create new guides, but the time is well spent if reading comprehension is improved.

French writer Guy de Maupassant's short stories are wonderful seminar text because, although de Maupassant's writing style is simplistic, his themes are complex and universal. From middle school to high school, students can read de Maupassant and enjoy the element of surprise in his stories. Figures 3.8 (p. 33), 3.9 (p. 34), 3.10 (p. 35), and 3.11 (p. 36) are teacher-created three-level study guides on four of de Maupassant's stories. Section I evaluates facts that are stated in the reading; section II requires students to draw conclusions without having an answer stated directly in the text; and section III asks for broad application of the text. Because of the brevity of each guide, students can finish a guide fairly quickly. Each guide, however, still achieves its purpose—causing students to think analytically.

Similar three-level study guides can be created for any seminar piece, fiction or nonfiction. Experience has shown these to be particularly helpful in broadening student thinking beyond the factual information. For seminar to be successful, thinking beyond the obvious is critical.

FIGURE 3.7. SEMINAR DIRECTED READING:
ACTIVITY 3: *All Quiet on the Western Front*

Directions: Find reference(s) to each item, give page numbers, and draw an inference about meaning.

Item	Page #'s	Inferences
1. Earth		
2. Front		
3. Government leaders		
4. Comradeship		
5. Cruelty		
6. Discipline		
7. Truth		
8. Propaganda		
9. Death		
10. Authority		
11. Training		
12. Weapons		
13. Youth		
14. Future		
15. Revenge		
16. War		
17. Emotions		
18. Dreams		
19. Fear		
20. Courage		
21. Food		
22. Enemies		
23. No Man's Land		
24. Trenches		
25. Peace		
26. Hope		
27. Generals		
28. Coffins		
29. Home		
30. Family		
Comments		

Figure 3.8. Three-Level Study Guide for "A Piece of String"

Check all correct responses.

Level I: Facts

___1. Monsieur Hauchecome is a poor man who saves things to use later.

___2. Monsieur Malandin finds the lost billfold.

___3. Hauchecome and Malandin have been friends for many years.

___4. After the wallet is found and returned, Hauchecome is treated with kindness and respect by the townspeople.

___5. The billfold is found, yet Hauchecome is still blamed.

Level II: Inferences

___1. The harness maker assumes Hauchecome picked up the wallet.

___2. Goderville citizens want to be forgiving and to believe in one's innocence.

___3. Hauchecome dies of a broken heart because he has been unjustly accused.

___4. Monsieur Malandin uses the situation to get revenge on Hauchecome.

___5. The people believe Hauchecome is guilty when he tries to prove his innocence.

Level III: Application

___1. Hauchecome's reputation is the only valuable possession he has.

___2. The truth is always more believable than a lie.

___3. When one is disbelieved, he feels the need to prove his innocence.

___4. Protesting against false accusations is interpreted as a sign of guilt.

___5. Hauchecome is a comic figure to the townspeople, but in reality his life is tragic.

FIGURE 3.9. THREE-LEVEL STUDY GUIDE FOR "THE NECKLACE"

Check the correct responses.

Level I: Facts

___1. Loisel gives his wife money to buy an expensive dress.

___2. Mme. Loisel borrows a valuable necklace from her friend.

___3. Loisel makes a great deal of money and is accustomed to taking his wife to fancy balls.

___4. Mme. Loisel works for twenty years to replace the lost necklace.

___5. Loisel refuses to help his wife pay for the necklace.

Level II: Inference

___1. Mme. Forestier is amused by Matilda's return of the necklace.

___2. Matilda is the belle of the ball because of her personality, not the necklace.

___3. Matilda's acceptance of the dress money shows her selfishness.

___4. Matilda doesn't really understand or appreciate her husband until she loses the necklace.

___5. After working to pay for the necklace, Matilda outward beauty is lost, but her inward character has improved.

Level III: Application

___1. Happiness comes from having possessions.

___2. Initially, poverty causes Matilda's selfishness and unappreciativeness.

___3. Hard work teaches one the true value of life.

___4. Pride and dignity come from hard work.

___5. One's behavior does not determine whether or not one is loved.

**FIGURE 3.10. THREE-LEVEL STUDY GUIDE FOR
"TWO FRIENDS"**

Check all correct responses.

Level I: Facts

___1. The two friends betray their country by revealing the password.

___2. The story is set in Germany in the 1900's.

___3. The France's enemy is Germany.

___4. The blockade of France has crippled the country.

___5. Without permission, the friends go fishing.

Level II: Inference

___1. The mood of the story is ominous.

___2. The blockade allowed for free movement from place to place.

___3. A true friendship doesn't need verbal communication, just shared interests.

___4. The German knew the men were really innocent of spying.

___5. Going fishing is an attempt to regain normalcy in their lives.

Level III: Application

___1. de Maupassant thinks the men deserve to die for the risks they take.

___2. Happiness is greater when one is able to regain a deprived pleasure.

___3. de Maupassant, the author, wants the reader to conclude that war makes men cruel and heartless.

___4. Military leaders have total disregard for human rights.

___5. Facing death without revealing secrets enables one to die heroically.

FIGURE 3.11. THREE-LEVEL STUDY GUIDE FOR "THE JEWELS"

Check the correct responses.

Level I: Facts

___1. Lantin believed he had married a virtuous woman.

___2. Lantin marries his wife for her wealth.

___3. The couple appears happy despite the interests they don't share.

___4. The wife's death is not unexpected.

___5. M. Lantin was proud of his wife's skill with money.

Level II: Inferences

___1. Society says a man is happier when he marries a virtuous woman.

___2. Lantin is embarrassed by his wife's flashy jewelry.

___3. Likely, Lantin's wife had been unfaithful to him on evenings he thought she was at the theater.

___4. Lantin's wife did not possess the money management qualities he attributed to her.

___5. Money and a virtuous second wife gave Lantin happiness.

Level III: Application

___1. Money solves all of life's problems.

___2. Spouses need to have a great deal in common.

___3. Reality is often different from appearances.

___4. Love is blind.

___5. The death of a loved one can sometimes make a person a better individual.

MARKING A TEXT

To become analytical readers who are prepared for seminar, students must mark their text. When "marking the text" is initially introduced to students, they get puzzled looks on their faces. Not surprising! While teachers may be from a generation where books were purchased and written in daily, today's students have been told to return their texts in pristine condition. Truly, marking the text for them is an anathema; consequently, they must be given instruction on how to mark their text.

Why do students need to mark their texts? Marking the text switches reading from a passive exercise to an active one. Even though short selections are usually used for seminar until students have learned seminar methods, later on they may be asked to read longer works of fiction and nonfiction that require considerable time and organizational skills. To quickly access a page, paragraph, or line in the work, students must be very familiar with the text. This familiarity does not come from hasty reading but arises from concentrated effort involving note-taking, reading activities, and marking of the text.

Marking the text requires the reader to underline, highlight, or take notes on ideas, issues, or themes in the work. The physical act of marking the text locks information into the student's memory and allows for retrieval of the material during seminar. Figure 3.12 (p. 38), which is adapted from Adler and Van Doren (1972), suggests various methods of marking a text.

How do students mark their text if they are allowed to write in them? This is a problem but not an insurmountable one. Very short selections can be copied for students; however, longer readings cannot be duplicated. Many teachers overcome this problem by supplying sticky notes to students. These adhere to the page and allow the student to make comments and notes. Other students cut slips of paper like bookmarks, placing them in the text and making notations on them. Once students understand the concept of marking the text, they find ways to compensate without defacing their textbooks.

GRAPHIC ORGANIZER MODELS

While directed reading activities, study guides, and marking the text serve many students well, other students are visual learners who prefer using charts or organizers to trace events or progression of ideas. For the majority of students, a combination of marking the text and using a visual is most effective. Failure, however, to produce any tangible preparation of the text is usually indicative of hasty, inadequate reading, invariably resulting in unsatisfactory seminar performance.

Figures 3.13 (p. 39) and 3.14 (p. 39) are graphic organizer models of reading activities for *The Awakening* and *The Grapes of Wrath*. Using a visual format for reading preparation is effective in part because students don't perceive they are doing the same amount of work when it appears on a chart or graphic organizer. The results are the same regardless of which reading models are used if students know the text and have processed the reading prior to seminar.

FIGURE 3.12. HOW TO MARK A BOOK

- Highlight or underline passages that reveal crucial information, that show changes in character, or that trace the development of character.
- Make notations in the margins as you react to passages that are unique or noteworthy.
- Place a question mark (?) in the margin if you don't understand what the passage means.
- Put an exclamation mark (!) in the margin to indicate something surprising or unusual.
- Consider using these symbols:
  - An asterisk (*) to emphasize a statement already underlined or to denote a recurring idea.
  - A plus sign (+) or (–) to indicate something you want to remember.
- Use sticky notes for marking major ideas, for cross-referencing ideas, or for easy access to specific pages in the text. Use a variety of colors.
- A smiling face (☺) shows you agree or like an idea.
- A frowning face (☹) shows disagreement or dislike.
- Circle keywords or phrases.
- Underline vocabulary words you don't know. Jot down a brief definition in the margin, especially if the word is critical to your understanding of the passage.

In the two models given here (Figs. 3.13 and 3.14), along with preparing for seminar, students are also prewriting for a processed paper that will follow the seminar. On the block schedule, teachers must utilize time well, maximizing every assignment. Whenever feasible in meeting objectives, one assignment is better than two because of the compressed time on block. As well, if reading activities are incorporated into other class requirements, students will give the tasks greater effort in both seminar and writing.

FIGURE 3.13. SEMINAR GRAPHIC ORGANIZER: *THE AWAKENING*

"Edna: A Role Model for Women or a Weak Woman?"

Edna's Strengths:

Page #	Strong qualities	Action that illustrates it

Edna's Weaknesses:

Page #	Weak qualities	Action that illustrates it

FIGURE 3.14. SEMINAR GRAPHIC ORGANIZER: *THE GRAPES OF WRATH*

"The Joads: Are they victims of circumstances or of an uncaring society?"

Page #	Quote	Causes or Influences on Joads

STUDENT READING GUIDES

In addition to reading, preparing the student for seminar requires reflection on the text before the actual seminar. The student can practice reflection by processing questions such as these: "What is the author's purpose in writing?" "What are five main ideas in the text?" "What can I learn from the way the character handles situations in his or her life?" "What relevance does the reading have to my life and the world in which I live?" By reflecting upon these questions or similar ones, students develop critical reading and thinking skills to analyze and sort information.

Figure 3.15 is a student reading guide that can be used in the seminar teaching process before the first seminar reading is assigned to students. Emphasis on reading and use of a variety of activities to strengthen reading skills is crucial to the overall success and enjoyment of seminar.

FIGURE 3.15. STUDENT READING GUIDE

- ◆ Read carefully for facts and ideas.
- ◆ Highlight intriguing and meaningful ideas.
- ◆ Make notes in the margins.
- ◆ Use sticky notes to mark pages or quotes.
- ◆ Prepare a note sheet or chart with main points and page references.
- ◆ Mark confusing passages.
- ◆ Ask for help with reading if needed.
- ◆ Reread the selection or read aloud with a parent.
- ◆ Look for connections between this work and other works.
- ◆ Reflect on the author's purpose.
- ◆ Bring the text and reading activities to the seminar.

Only the student who has read and mentally prepared is a strong seminar participant. If the teacher is to find success using the seminar strategy, all efforts must be taken to insure that students read and prepare in depth. The rewards are worth the effort for everyone. By using the seminar and well-constructed activities, the teacher is able to cover material more efficiently whether on the block or a traditional schedule. For students, there is no other experience that compares to the intellectual stimulation and opportunity for self-expression that comes with a seminar.

REFERENCES

Adler, M. J., and Van Doren, C. (1972). *How to Read a Book.* New York: Simon & Schuster.

Richardson, , and Morgan, , *Reading to Learn in the Content Areas.*

4

TEXT SELECTION

Pacing guides and long-range planning are part of every teacher's preparation for a new school year, especially with recent shifts to block scheduling and compressed class time. Before students ever report to class, teachers scan their curriculum, determining what teaching strategy is most suited to the material and what strategy will best achieve desired outcomes. One effective strategy is the Socratic Seminar. While not everything can be taught using the seminar—few strategies are all-inclusive—but incorporating seminars into classes once a week or every other week infuses the classroom with vitality and enthusiasm.

Selection of seminar readings, which come from all disciplines—including science, literature, art, history, mathematics, vocational, and philosophy—is made easier because most schools have a clearly defined course of study and specific objectives that must be met. Selecting works that are already embedded in the curriculum which lend themselves to the seminar strategy is advised. In most classes using the seminar will not add additional readings; instead, seminars cover required curriculum in a more interesting and efficient way. In subjects that have been taught more didactically with slight regard to establishing relevance, additional readings must be added for the seminar process. Seminars do not minimize the importance of factual information but emphasize making sense of the data and applying it to the world. Certainly, acquisition and application of knowledge are equally important for students.

GUIDELINES FOR DETERMINING
THE SUITABILITY OF TEXTS

Several guidelines should be observed in determining whether a text is suitable for an effective seminar. Is the text filled with issues and ideas worthy of discussion? Will the text sustain discussion and allow for extended exploration of concepts? Does the text include complexities, ambiguities, contradictions, or mysteries, which offer several possible interpretations of issues? A text that does not meet these requirements should be taught by another method, not as a seminar.

♦ Is the text worthy of discussion?

Every instructor should consider this question before requiring students to read anything. In other words, what ideas are embedded in the text that relate to students' lives? If the selection is used for pure reading comprehension, the reading skills and thinking involved are quite different from what is being asked for on a seminar reading. Seminar pieces require the student to think critically and to consider all the possibilities and consequences as opposed to looking solely for right or wrong answers. A selection worthy of discussion allows students to make connections with life. When relevance to life is apparent, both interest levels and critical thinking are enhanced.

♦ Will the text sustain discussion and allow for exploration of concepts? How long should students talk about one piece?

The length of the selection often determines the answer. A short fable probably will not sustain discussion for as long as Sophocles' *Antigone* will, which is filled with rich ideas and real-world relevance. Similarly, a seminar on *The Scarlet Letter* can last for several hours, whereas a newspaper article about the shaming angle in the American judicial system may not sustain discussion for as long. Both selections are equally valuable, but the time allotted to seminar will differ.

♦ Does the text include complexities, ambiguities, contradictions, or mysteries that offer several possible interpretations of issues?

When a selection has obvious facts that cannot be extended, it is not a suitable seminar text. Again, consider *Antigone*. There are no simple explanations for Antigone's, Creon's, or Haemon's actions and decisions. Everything is complicated and interwoven with each character's actions somehow affecting everyone else's. As well, the issues are universal—obeying God's or man's laws, keeping a king's power under control, taking advice from one's children, accepting responsibility for one's actions, respecting women and the dead, and standing strong for one's beliefs. There are no simple right or wrong answers, and the decisions made by characters are complex and controversial. Students can talk at length about *Antigone*, documenting their comments with textual evidence and relating their own experiences to Antigone's life. After having participated in a seminar, students can never forget *Antigone!*

STRATEGIES FOR TEXT SELECTION

It is important to remember that the purpose of seminar is not to teach facts or to coach skills. The seminar text, therefore, is not pure science, but the ethics of science; not mathematical computation, but the theory and usefulness of math; not the chapter on the causes of World War I, but Remarque's *All Quiet on the Western Front*. For example, while the textbook chapter is not suited for seminar text, the sidebars included for enrichment may be marvelous readings, ideally suited for seminar. As well, teacher editions have listings of additional readings to accompany each unit, and many of these meet the requirements for a seminar text. Seminar texts may be taken from a variety of sources. Genres include plays, poems, sermons, stories, essays, novels, films, art, and music.

COMBINED READINGS

Because learning does not occur in isolation, teachers should look for opportunities to combine related readings, which are usually referred to as paired readings or companion readings. For example, in *Cry, the Beloved Country,* Jarvis is inspired deeply by "The Gettysburg Address" and quotes a line from the speech; consequently, it is logical to have students discuss Lincoln's writing along with the novel. Without an understanding of the two pieces, Jarvis' admiration of Lincoln is totally lost. In middle school, teachers can combine poems and short stories with similar or contrasting themes to give students a more comprehensive understanding of the material. Often, the readings for younger students are quite brief and limited in scope. Paired readings can give the seminar more depth and breadth, thus encouraging and sustaining critical thinking. For example, combining the short story "Charles" with Phyllis McGinley's poem "Lament of the Normal Child" allows students to explore two different scenarios in which children confront the educational system. By pairing these pieces, the range of discussion is extended. Figure 4.1 gives examples of paired readings.

FIGURE 4.1. PAIRED SEMINAR READINGS

♦ "George to George"—Inaugural addresses of Presidents Washington and Bush

♦ "The Battle of Finney's Ford" with "The Enemy"—West's and Buck's short stories from the Revolutionary War and World War II.

♦ Songs protesting war with *All Quiet on the Western Front*—similar themes about war.

♦ *The Canterbury Tales* with the film *Beckett* (starring Richard Burton and Peter O'Toole)—provides background for the reading of Chaucer.

♦ "How Much Land Does a Man Need" with a current article on materialism in the United States.

♦ Two articles—pro and con—on the tobacco debate—recommended for health or history classes.

♦ "Bill of Rights" with articles on gun control, freedom of speech, and so forth.

In selecting paired readings, teachers should first check for themes that span time and geographic borders. Then, they should decide which readings logically connect and extend the learning. Combining related texts causes students to consider the same concepts in a broader framework. Ironically, a byproduct of companion readings is efficiency of coverage for the teacher. If related issues and themes can be discussed in one sitting, valuable class time is saved, which can be used for process writing or research. Art and film can also be powerful seminar texts, especially when combined with a short reading.

USING ARTWORKS AS TEXTS

Pictures which students in the past may have ignored altogether suddenly are observed and analyzed for meaning. For instance, Frederick Douglas's essay "What the Black Man Wants" and his short story "The Battle with Mr. Covey" are good seminar pieces alone or paired; however, they are even more intriguing when joined with the artwork "Slaves Escaping through the Swamp." Prior experience with these pieces in seminar has shown that students have focused more heavily on the art instead of the readings, discussing the colors, lighting, dogs, and so forth. Oddly enough, inferences drawn from the art have been more insightful than those evoked by the essay or short story. Without the painting's inclusion as a seminar text, however, students may have passed over it in their anthology without a second glance.

Even lower elementary students without strong reading skills can discuss art intelligently. For example, an art teacher reported that her third graders discussed a picture of old-fashioned gasoline pumps for a full 45 minutes. Other teachers have commented on discussions of familiar fables where the art played a significant role. If the same piece is discussed, but the illustrator is different, students rely on the pictures for their inferences about characters' economic status and personalities. Undeniably, regardless of age, students are heavily influenced by the visual; consequently, incorporating art into seminar is encouraged.

USING FILMS AS TEXTS

Viewing is a learning strand in the North Carolina Communications Curriculum, K–12. Viewing, however, involves considerably more than simply watching a movie. The goal is for students to acquire knowledge, be critical viewers, and make connections between the printed word and the visual. Seminars on films can help with these objectives. Films work best for seminar if students have been given a viewing task that focuses them on the movie. As well, completion of the task gives them a product to have on their desks for reference and documentation during the seminar. For instance, students may watch *The Glass Menagerie* in preparation for seminar. First, before seeing the film, the class should have read the play independently so that the content is familiar to them. During the viewing, ask students to list the major characters and any actions or statements they make that are revealing of their personalities and motivations. In addition, have students note themes, issues, or controversial incidents that may have significance. While the teacher is not highlighting specific points for taking notes, she is setting up a framework for concentrated viewing. Conducting seminars on film is an excellent way to teach critical viewing skills to students who have been bombarded by media. Unfortunately, they have seen so much that they passively watch without thinking significantly; the seminar can break that cycle.

Students may use the chart in Figure 4.2 to extract information from the film and to focus their viewing on characters, issues, themes, and incidents that may be particularly important to discuss in seminar. Without a task or focused viewing, students tend to "zone out" while watching films. To discuss a film in seminar, students must have attuned and taken notes to use later. Critical viewing guides should also be used when students watch nonfiction films, especially if a seminar is to follow.

FIGURE 4.2. SEMINAR VIEWING GUIDE

List themes, issues, incidents, and inferences about characters' motivations. Use this list for documentation of contributions made in seminar.

Themes:	Issues:
Incidents:	Inferences:

MATH TEXTS

Although text selection may not be as readily available for math as for English, history, or science, math students need to talk about the relevance of their studies, too. Even a discussion of technology in the math classroom can make for an enlightening seminar. Magazine articles and professional journals are good sources for readings. Short stories such as Asimov's "The Feeling of Power" relate directly to math. In "The Feeling of Power," Asimov envisions a society dependent on computers, where citizens have forgotten how to do basic math. When an insignificant man rediscovers this skill, the struggles ensue. Every math student would benefit from talking about Asimov's predictions and moral dilemmas. Also, drawings and objects work well as math texts. For example, a blueprint for a home is an excellent starting point for students to discuss math skills needed to build a house. The application of skills translates to greater retention and motivation. Other texts can work equally well for seminar, and while seminars may not occur as frequently in math as in other reading-based courses, students remember information they have connected to their own lives.

SOURCES OF SEMINAR TEXTS

Seminar texts are everywhere—anthologies, history books, and primary documents, illustrations, newspapers, and magazines. When planning, teachers should first evaluate what they already teach for seminar readings before searching for other sources. Remember that teachers should use the seminar to teach their curriculum; they should not make additional requirements unless elements of the curriculum need greater depth and enrichment.

Figure 4.3 is a list of texts that have been used by teachers in various disciplines. While an all-inclusive list is not possible, the texts provided here may generate ideas for other texts.

FIGURE 4.3. SAMPLE SEMINAR TEXTS

Poems

- "Dreams," "The Dream Keeper," "Dream Deferred," "I, Too," "Harlem," and "Mother to Son"—Langston Hughes
- Poetry about anger: "A Poison Tree"—William Blake
- "Oh, Oh, You Will Be Sorry for That Word"—Millay
- "The Heart"—Stephen Crane
- "The Black Panther"—John Hall Wheelock
- "Richard Cory"—Robinson
- "The Road Not Taken"—Robert Frost
- "I Will Fight No More"—Chief Joseph

Short Stories

- "Report on the Barnhouse Effect"—Kurt Vonnegut
- "The Feeling of Power"—Isaac Asimov
- "The Devil and Tom Walker"—Washington Irving
- "The Devil and Daniel Webster"—Stephen Vincent Benet
- "No Witchcraft for Sale"—Doris Lessing
- "The Overcoat"—Nikolai Gogol
- "How Much Land Does a Man Need"—Leo Tolstoy
- "The Artist" and "The Man from Kabul"—Tagore
- "The Boar Hunt"—Jose Vasconcelos
- "The Bet"—Anton Chekhov
- "Charles" and "The Lottery"—Shirley Jackson
- "To Build a Fire"—Jack London
- "A Horseman in the Sky"—Ambrose Bierce
- "Your Place is Empty Now'—Anne Tyler
- "Field Trip"—Tim O'Brian
- "Lamb to the Slaughter"—Roald Dahl
- "The Necklace"—Guy de Maupassant
- "The Interlopers"—Saki
- "The Needle" and "The Key"—Isaac Bashevis Singer
- "The Rat Trap"—Selma Lagerlof
- "Rappaccini's Daughter"—Nathaniel Hawthorne
- "The Use of Force"—William Carlos Williams
- "Manhood"—John Wain
- "The Battle With Mr. Covey"—Frederick Douglas

Essays

- "We Aren't Superstitious"—Stephen Vincent Benet
- from *Self-Reliance*—Ralph Waldo Emerson
- "Woman in the Nineteenth Century"—Margaret Fuller
- from *Resistance to Civil Government*—Henry David Thoreau
- "What Is an American?"—Jean de Crevecoeur
- "The Earth Does Not Belong to Man"—Chief Seattle
- "This Sacred Soil"—Chief Seattle
- "Concerning the Savages of North America"—Ben Franklin

- Selections from *Common Sense*—Thomas Paine
- "The Apology"—Plato
- "What the Black Man Wants"—Frederick Douglas
- "Law of Human Nature"—C. S. Lewis
- "On Geometry and Experience" from *Evolution of Physics*—Albert Einstein
- Excerpts from *The Origins of the Species*—Charles Darwin
- "Concerning Probability" from *The World of Mathematics*
- *Flatland: A Romance of Many Dimensions*—Edwin A. Abbott
- Arguments for and against Galileo from *The Defense of Galileo*
- Excerpts from *On the Revolutions of Heavenly Spheres*
- *Dora: An Analysis of a Case of Hysteria*—Sigmund Freud
- Excerpts from *Elements*—Euclid
- Excerpts from *Science and Method*—Poincare

Novels

- *Cry, The Beloved Country*—Alan Paton
- *One Day in the Life of Ivan Denisovich*—Alexander Solzhenitsyn
- *The Chosen*—Chaim Potok
- *A Separate Peace*—John Knowles
- *To Kill a Mockingbird*—Harper Lee
- *Their Eyes Were Watching God*—Zora Neale Hurston
- *Lord of the Flies*—William Golding
- *Deathwatch*—Robb White
- *Frankenstein*—Mary Shelley
- *The Great Gatsby*—F. Scott Fitzgerald
- *The Grapes of Wrath*—John Steinbeck
- *The Moon Is Down*—John Steinbeck
- *The Old Man and the Sea*—Ernest Hemingway
- *Ethan Frome*—Edith Wharton
- *Wuthering Heights*—Bronte
- *Silas Marner*—Elliot
- *The Red Badge of Courage*—Stephen Crane
- *All Quiet on the Western Front*—Erich Remarque
- *The Scarlet Letter*—Nathaniel Hawthorne

Sermons/Speeches

- ♦ "Speech to the Virginia Assembly"—Patrick Henry
- ♦ "Sinners in the Hands of an Angry God"—Jonathan Edwards
- ♦ "I Have a Dream"—Martin Luther King
- ♦ "George to George"—Washington's and Bush's Inaugural Addresses
- ♦ "One Great Heart"—Alexander Solzhenitsyn
- ♦ "Pericles' Funeral Oration"—Thucydides

Articles

- ♦ "Uranium Bound for Japan in 1945 Complicates Bomb Debate"— *The Herald-Sun*, Durham, NC (12/21/95)
- ♦ "Hiroshima: The Aftershocks"—*US News and World Report* (7/31/95)
- ♦ "Immigration: Who Belongs? Who Decides?"—*Scholastic Update* (11/95)
- ♦ "The Last Days of Auschwitz"—*Newsweek* (1/16/95)
- ♦ "Paying for Crime with Shame"—*USA Today* (6/12/97)
- ♦ "The Name of the Game is Shame"—*Newsweek* (6/12/94)
- ♦ "Cheating Hearts, Mixed Feelings"—*USA Today* (12/12/97)
- ♦ "Attitudes on Adultery"—*USA Today* (6/12/97)

Fables

- ♦ "The Lion and the Mouse," "The Frogs Desiring a King," and "The Town Mouse and the Country Mouse"—from *Aesop's Fable*
- ♦ "Numskull and the Rabbit"—from the *Panchatantra*
- ♦ "Sibi"—from the *Mahabharata*
- ♦ "A Fable"—Mark Twain

Dramas

- ♦ *Medea*—Euripides
- ♦ *Antigone*—Sophocles
- ♦ *A Doll's House*—Henrik Ibsen
- ♦ *Our Town*—Thornton Wilder
- ♦ *The Glass Menagerie*—Tennessee Williams
- ♦ *The Crucible*—Arthur Miller
- ♦ *Twelve Angry Men*—Reginald Rose

Art

- ◆ "Slaves Escaping Though the Swamp"
- ◆ "Relativity"—Eischer
- ◆ *World Masterpieces* transparency series—Prentice Hall Literature

Film

- ◆ *Inherit the Wind*—Robert Lee
- ◆ *Green Cows, Quaggas, and Mummies*
- ◆ *Beckett*

Satire

- ◆ "A Modest Proposal"—Jonathan Swift
- ◆ "My Melancholy Face"—Heinrich Boll
- ◆ "Action Will Be Taken"—Heinrich Boll
- ◆ "The Happy Man"—Najib Mahfouz
- ◆ "School vs. Education"—Russell Baker

Nonfiction

- ◆ *Night*—Elie Weisel
- ◆ "Arriving at Moral Perfection"—Ben Franklin
- ◆ *The Declaration of Independence*—Thomas Jefferson
- ◆ Selections from *The Federalist Papers*—James Madison
- ◆ "The Letter 'A'"—Christy Brown
- ◆ *Having Our Say*—the Delaney sisters with Amy Hearth
- ◆ Salem Court Documents of 1692
- ◆ *Silent Spring*—Rachel Carson

5

APPLYING SEMINARS TO THE DISCIPLINES

What characteristics does society and the workplace want in students as they complete their education? Consider these attributes: knowledge; ethics; responsibility; enthusiasm; integrity; dependability; adaptability; respect for others; communication and decision-making skills; and a willingness to continue learning for a lifetime. Aren't these the traits all students and employees should possess?

What society and the workplace want are synonymous with what teachers want, but where do students learn all of these skills and behaviors? From all of life and school experiences, of course, but how do educators set up a framework to address this challenge of educating the total person? First, by accepting that change is inevitable, and second, by creating a positive school and classroom climate to foster effective teaching and rigorous curricula. What do these positive climates have in common?

According to the 1995 report of the North Carolina Accountability Commission, schools with positive climates share these traits:

- A supportive, stimulating environment
- Student-centered
- Positive expectations
- Provides feedback
- Rewards good performance
- A sense of family
- Closeness to parents and community
- Lines of communication are always open
- Focus on achievement
- Trust

Across the nation, not just in North Carolina, educational leadership and teachers are searching for ways to better meet the needs of students and of a technologically advanced society. Jobs once available to unskilled laborers have

51

vanished, and without the attributes listed previously, students struggle to find meaningful employment. How does this affect schools and teachers? Society and the workplace look to educators to find ways to equip students to not only survive but thrive.

To meet the needs of students, teachers must incorporate strategies which tap the total person and who he is—his values and attitudes, his goals and dreams, and his potential as a lifelong learner and citizen. No one strategy can satisfy the demands; instead, combinations of proven strategies must be utilized K–12. Socratic Seminars, by design, address elements of what society says is vital for its youth to have upon completion of school. While these characteristics are never consciously taught through seminar, the framework allows students to explore the text, to share their belief systems, to show tolerance for opposing views, to integrate their learning in various subjects, to attach real life relevance to each topic, and to become more effective communicators verbally and written. All of this exploration of the text is occurring in an atmosphere where trust and respect are valued and enforced, where diversity is encouraged, and where intellectual growth is stimulated.

In a sense, students of varying abilities are learning from each other in seminar. One student is not teaching the other, however. They all come out gaining because learning has been the priority. In initial seminars, students are in for an eye-opening experience as they realize how many interpretations one issue may have, how "right and wrong" answers are not paramount in the seminar, but how the goal is to uncover and document the many possibilities. Students have described their initial experiences as "refreshing and invigorating," and as "real learning which is more than a good grade." If seminars can evoke these feelings in students, should not every teacher add this strategy to his bag of tricks?

Why then are seminars not applied to all the disciplines? Research indicates that American schools do a better job of imparting information than in teaching application of that knowledge. When United States students are compared internationally, their knowledge of content is strong; however, Asia and Europe increasingly emphasize the application of acquired knowledge. American students, according to William Daggett, a renowned educational reformer, are not faring well at the higher levels where they must apply knowledge within or between disciplines and to real-world predictable and unpredictable problems.

The mandate and challenge are clear: give students the essential skills in every discipline to move into the higher levels of thinking and application. While application of knowledge may be harder to test and evaluate, students must have application to be employable; consequently, schools and teaching strategies must prepare students for the world in which they live. Dialogue, which is the key ingredient of seminar, is an essential part of the equation. Teachers must not merely cover material, but they must teach it in an interdisciplinary framework. The guiding question becomes the difference between knowing and understanding. While "thoughtless mastery" may suffice in some classroom settings, it doesn't work in seminar where thought, relevance, and understanding are paramount goals.

Teachers cite other reasons, such as planning time constraints and state testing programs, for not universally using seminars across the disciplines; however, research indicates that these barriers must be removed. Meeting the needs of students supercedes any challenges of implementation. Although team-teaching may not always be feasible or even desirable, making connections and applications within a discipline is always possible.

For example, when students study world literature in tenth grade, the teacher's hope is that they will retain knowledge of key themes, characters, and cultures. The following term in American literature, students should make linkages in seminar to these issues from the previous course. If the ideas are analogous, then the ideas should transcend curricular restraints. Intense joy should be the English teacher's emotion when a student says, "This reminds me of what we studied in biology last week." Why? Without any direct solicitation from the seminar facilitator, the student has integrated his learning, making connections that affirm the validity of what is being taught in both English and biology. How awesome, but regrettably, how rare an experience. By incorporating seminar across the disciplines, however, those awesome moments that remind us of why we became teachers occur more frequently.

SUGGESTIONS FOR AN INTEGRATED SEMINAR UNIT

How should teachers apply seminars to the disciplines? One suggestion is to plan an integrated unit with the seminar as the culminating event. For example, a unit could be designed around Darwinism, creationism, John Scopes, the "Monkey Trials," *Inherit the Wind*, and man's right to think for himself in a democratic society. Realistically, this unit should encompass science, history, and English, but it may involve other curriculum areas as well. After examining the historical and scientific backgrounds and learning any necessary factual information, the students are ready to read Lawrence and Lee's drama *Inherit the Wind*, and to come together for seminar, where the text can be explored from many perspectives, not just a literary one. This teaming approach demonstrates the interconnectedness of learning across the disciplines. Some specific possibilities in different disciplines are suggested in the balance of this chapter.

HISTORY

- Present information and reading about controversy surrounding Tennessee teacher John Scopes and his challenge to the state law that restricted any teaching of Darwin in public schools. Discuss his reasons for the challenge and how his choice affected his life. Study and discuss the attorneys in the actual trial and how they impacted historical events.

- Research the beginnings of the Civil Liberties Union and how that organization was involved in the "Monkey Trials." Discuss the cultural and religious climate of small town Tennessee at the time of the trial.

♦ Read *Inherit the Wind* for culminating seminar and prepare pre-seminar task. The preseminar task is to list differences and similarities between the historical account of the trial and the fictionalized one in the play. Figure 5.1 is a preseminar chart that may be used for this purpose.

SCIENCE

♦ Introduce the concept of Darwinism versus creationism, using the chapter in the science text.

♦ Discuss both positions, telling the class that they must decide the issue for themselves based on their individual consciences.

♦ Read articles that support both sides so that students have a balanced view.

♦ Schedule a short seminar on the articles, but stress that all comments made in the seminar must be documented by the text. Because the issue deals with religion, assess your climate to know if this is a safe seminar topic. If not, turn the seminar opening and closing questions into writings. Later, share excerpts from the writings with the class.

♦ On a graphic organizer, chart the best scientific arguments for and against each position. In small groups, share out your arguments and compare them to others in the group. Make a list of the best arguments and list this on a chart to be posted for entire class review.

♦ Read *Inherit the Wind* for culminating seminar with English and history students.

♦ Complete the preseminar chart for *Inherit the Wind* given in Figure 5.2 (p. 56). Chart Matthew Brady's argument for creationism and Henry Drummond's argument for evolution. Remember to tell students the point value of the preseminar task. (Chapter 6 provides additional information on preseminar tasks.)

FIGURE 5.1. HISTORY PRESEMINAR CHART

Date: _____   Student: _____

History Preseminar Chart: *Inherit the Wind*

Similarities between history and fiction:

Historical Records   **Play**

Differences between history and fiction:

History   **Play**

FIGURE 5.2. SCIENCE PRESEMINAR TASK SHEET

Date: _____   Student: _____

Science Preseminar Chart: *Inherit the Wind*

A. Matthew Brady's Arguments for Creationism

B. Henry Drummond's Arguments for Evolution

ENGLISH

♦ Have students read *Inherit the Wind* silently or aloud in class, dramatizing the story.

♦ Discuss vocabulary words that may be unfamiliar to students such as heretic, fundamentalism, and so forth.

♦ In small groups, prepare charts of descriptive words for various characters in the play. Post these around the room.

♦ Select a character and using his name listed vertically, write a bio-poem using the first letter of his name as a starting point for each line. Look at the posted charts for ideas.

♦ Have students prepare a list of issues in addition to creationism and evolution that are discussed in the play. Have them save this list to use in seminar.

♦ For an in-class writing, ask students to describe the character with whom they most identify, most dislike, most respect, or find most intriguing. Suggest an appropriate format and length for the writing.

♦ Creative writing in class—ask students to select a particular scene from *Inherit the Wind* and rewrite the scene to match their own wishes for the character.

♦ The preseminar task for the culminating event is to write an essay on one particular theme, other than evolution or creationism, in the play. Answer questions such as length, format, and scoring for the seminar task.

♦ *Caution:* In completing the in-class activities, be careful not to discuss the actual content of the play. If this occurs, the freshness of the seminar is lost.

ADDITIONAL SEMINAR SUGGESTIONS

When seminars are applied in specific subjects, there are tremendous opportunities for enhanced communication and real-world relevance. These suggestions may be useful for seminars:

♦ **United States History:** Bill of Rights and articles on gun control or freedom of speech. Be sure to include for and against positions.

♦ **World History and World Literature:** *Medea* and an article or list detailing how the Greeks perceived themselves as a superior culture.

♦ **English:** The film *Beckett* for seminar before studying *The Canterbury Tales*.

♦ **Math or Vocational Education:** Use of house blueprint to identify math skills involved in building the structure.

- **Chemistry:** Discuss articles about the effects of chemical additives in food or the effects of chemicals on the environment.
- **Vocational:** Discuss articles dealing with the changing workplace, the retraining of workers, and the technological demands of the next century.
- **Computer Science:** Discuss Isaac Asimov's "The Feeling of Power," which depicts the future and the dangers of dependency on computers.
- **Health:** Find texts on stress and its effects on the individual.
- **Nutrition:** Discuss various diets and whether they are nutritionally sound.
- **Art, English, or Science:** Discuss Loren Eiseley's "The Bird and the Machine," in which he assesses the value of both.

There are many choices of text for seminar, but perhaps those listed will spur teachers to look for obvious linkages which they often present to the students, but which the students rarely have time to discuss in depth.

Middle school teams and elementary teachers can also use seminar for integrated lessons as they tackle objectives such as teaching reading skills, understanding historical or scientific significance, strengthening social interaction and communication, and broadening multiculturalism. All of these goals can be addressed in seminar through appropriate readings. A universal theme in many cultures is "how humans got fire." By reading myths from various cultures, students can compare their reasoning, scientific knowledge, and belief systems. Hopefully, they will begin to see the similarities and not just differences.

Sometimes teachers use short fables or other readings to introduce a lesson. Because the purpose is to jumpstart thinking, only a brief time may be allotted to the seminar. When a longer, sustained discussion is needed, the teacher should add an article, essay, or short story that explores related issues. An introductory seminar serves well in eliciting what students know, believe, and want to know.

VARIOUS WAYS A SINGLE TEXT MAY BE APPLIED TO DIFFERENT DISCIPLINES

The classic fable "Town Mouse and Country Mouse" is applicable to many disciplines. Here are some suggestions for adapting the fable to specific teaching situations:

- Health, PE, Science

  You are teaching a lesson on stress management. Develop questions that enable students to discuss how on person's happiness may cause another person's stress.

- ◆ Health, PE, Science

  You are teaching a lesson about stress and how different things can cause stress depending on the individual. Discuss how the mice reacted to their stress.

- ◆ English, History

  You are teaching a lesson about how one's individual perspective on an event or issue can affect the decisions made and the outcomes of those decisions. Focus on the two ways the mice view life and environment differently.

- ◆ Home Economics, Health, Sociology

  You are teaching a lesson on nutrition and food choices. What connections can you draw between choice of food, lifestyle, behavioral, and environmental factors associated with food? Develop questions that cause students to explore these issues.

- ◆ Elementary, Middle School

  You are working with students on social skills, personal interactions, and friendship-building. Focus on qualities of friendship.

- ◆ Elementary, Middle School

  You want students to come to appreciate their home communities, yet to learn, with an open mind, about people who choose to live in drastically different circumstances.

- ◆ Social Studies, Sociology

  You are learning about historical migrations to cities and away from cities. Focus on why migrations occur.

- ◆ English

  You are preparing to teach a unit on American Romanticism and the characteristics of this period, including distrust of city life.

- ◆ Art
  - • Requires two versions of "The Town Mouse and the Country Mouse" with different illustrators.

  You are teaching a lesson about how readers are influenced by different illustrations of the same written text. Give half the group one illustrated text and the other half a text by another illustrator. Develop questions that cause them to draw conclusions based on both the text and the illustrations.

Seminar is a successful strategy when applied across the disciplines. While the frequency of use may vary, the benefits of seminar are the same—increased interest, better communication skills, and stronger relevance as students move to the higher levels of applying what they have learned.

6

WRITING SOCRATIC QUESTIONS

"We often search for better answers when we should be searching for better questions."

The greatest challenge for most Socratic seminar leaders is the writing of thought-provoking questions that fit some unique standards. The process begins with the teacher's own careful reading and marking of the text and a listing of all issues and ideas that should be explored in a rich and thorough discussion. The next step is translating this list into a series of questions designed to generate discussion of most of the ideas, which may be constructed in any order, but which are delivered in sequential order: opening, core, and closing.

OPENING QUESTIONS

This is the first, and also the broadest, question asked. Its purpose is to send the class directly to the text in any number of places for evidence. It should solicit the most far reaching variety of responses that engage the class for 15–45 minutes or more, depending on the length of text or the maturity of the class. It should never have a single or even finite list of responses because the question is on a mission of understanding, of teasing out the fabric and texture of text, not of highlighting facts.

If the question is to work well, it should meet several other criteria. First, it should avoid "yes" or "no" answers unless the rhetorical "why" would follow the question. The forced choice of "yes" or "no" and its subsequent defense may be a powerful tool for setting up profound ideas, particularly if elements of both choices may be defended.

Second, an opening question should be provocative and compelling, immediately engaging the mind and sending the eye to the text. Language is selected deliberately to invite thinking and should never sound like a teacher test discussion question. Every student should be able to comprehend every word of the question.

61

Third, and probably the most difficult to accomplish, the question should be "value" free. That is, it should contain no judgment words that might indicate the teacher's, or author's, position. A seminar leader must remain neutral in questioning, matching the neutrality of body language and facial expressions. All judgments, deductions, and connections must be made by students if they are to feel truly responsible for the seminar.

To push the idea of value- or judgment-free questions just a bit further is to propose a strange mandate and seeming contradiction: write a question that engages and compels but really contains no ideas at all because all ideas should come from students. Just how is this accomplished?

Let's assume that the seminar piece is the ancient play *Medea*. On the preparatory list of ideas the teacher hopes will be explored are the themes of vengeance and jealousy. But to write the opening question, "How do the themes of jealousy and vengeance trace through *Medea*?" is to focus the discussion fairly narrowly on teacher-identified topics. This limits what will be discussed and keeps the teacher in a power position over what is worth talking about. In addition, to use the word "theme" dilutes the provocative nature of the question. "Theme" is a teacher word, not a thinking word.

Better openings that may still lead to vengeance and jealousy are:

◆ "From the title, one might suppose that all roads lead to Medea. What is her impact on others in the play?"

◆ "There are many characters in the play, but the title is *Medea*. Why?"

◆ "What is Medea's role in the different relationships of her life?"

◆ "Someone said there are three types of people in the world: those who make things happen, those who watch things happen, and those who ask, 'What happened?' Which is Medea, and why?"

Note that two of the questions have a "setup" statement to pique the students' thinking without really giving them ideas. The questions are really quite similar in their focus on the character of Medea as a jumping-in point without establishing what her character is like.

These questions nudge thinking, like a gentle poke in the side, as opposed to "How is Medea a bitter vengeful wretch?", which is a teacher-delivered two-by-four over the head. Students own the former questions because they determine the direction and flow of the response. Teachers own the latter question, controlling the talk and reaching the destination before students have taken the trip!

OK, so the teacher still wants to ensure that vengeance and jealousy get on the boards? Another approach to an opening question is to conduct a round robin. Students are asked to reflect a few moments and jot down a word or phrase to complete the following statement: "*Medea* is really a play about _____." (Isn't this really calling for "theme" without using the word?) After all have completed the task, the teacher goes around the circle with each student contributing a word or phrase to fill in the blank. These are recorded on the board or on an overhead where all can see.

Now, teacher, it is fair game to say, "Mary and Charles both say *Medea* is really about vengeance. Is it?" (Rhetorical yes or no and then why?) The teacher may now use this judgment word "vengeance" because it is student introduced. And note, too, that the teacher doesn't ask "How is it a play of vengeance?" because that clearly indicates the teacher's approval on vengeance as a theme. "*Is it* about vengeance, as Mary and Charles indicate?" floats their idea but keeps the facilitator neutral. Anytime students introduce an idea, that idea is fair game for translation into a teacher question, as long as the student, not the teacher, is credited with the idea.

Opening questions may be as broad as, "What's going on in this play?", or, to make it even more user-friendly, "What's with this Medea woman?" This example, in familiar colloquial style, helps to break down the barrier that more erudite wording, such as, "What are the internal motivations of the essential character in *Medea*?", may create. Because the opening question can make or break the seminar, teachers should give special attention to choosing language that is neither sterile nor fancy. In fact, it is useful to write two opening questions in case one falls flat. The additional one may be tapped as a broader core question. Keep the opening simple, fresh, and unpredictable!

An excellent opening on John Hersey's *Hiroshima* is, "Typically, we think of light as something positive, invigorating, a point of clarity. 'I saw the light.' What is the light in *Hiroshima*?" Students often sit in stunned silence, taking in the question for a few moments before answering. They could not have predicted that question. And that is the challenge for seminar leaders—to find fresh provocative questions and never ever use the same question more than once a year!

CORE QUESTIONS

After the opening question has been thoroughly explored, the teacher asks a series of "core" questions. These should sustain discussion for 5–15 minutes each, which is less than the opening because they are more focused on finite issues and subtext. Depending on the length and complexity of the reading, three to eight cores should be composed to get at more content- specific ideas.

Often a key passage, line, or phrase is identified for interpretation. In "The Gettysburg Address," core questions may be:

♦ "What does Lincoln mean by 'of the people, by the people, and for the people?'"

♦ "What is meant by 'the unfinished work' in line 13?" (When citing a particular line of text for explanation, it is useful to give students the line number for reference.)

Core questions also examine central points and may begin or end with "how" or "why." An example from "The Gettysburg Address" is, "Lincoln uses some form of the term 'dedicate' six times in the speech. Why is this?" In none of the examples are ideas forwarded or teacher points of view expressed. Students are simply nudged with one finger to become the sense makers. Teachers merely point the way but do not take them to the destination.

Core questions are generated more directly from the teacher's preparatory listing of ideas and issues for the text. They cause students to concentrate on one issue until it has been discussed in depth. The quality of the leader's question directly determines how much and how deeply the text is explored and to what extent the teacher lesson objectives are covered in seminar.

A real challenge is to word the cores in such a way that to answer them will highlight issues the teacher cannot state in the question. Again, in "The Gettysburg Address," the teacher has listed some key quotes on the preparation sheet:

- ◆ "all men are created equal"
- ◆ "full measure of devotion"
- ◆ not "dying in vain"
- ◆ "new birth of freedom"

But rather than going for each as a core question, she wrote," What was Lincoln's vision in the speech?", and then only asked a core on the passages above that were not covered by her more encompassing question.

Keen listening is required on many fronts in becoming a good seminar leader. It is a critical skill, however, to listen for students who cover the ideas of one or more core questions in the broad, sweeping net of directions students take on the opening question. Seminar leaders take great pleasure in marking through their cores as these questions are examined without being asked.

Good seminar leaders also listen for students who hint at or introduce a core question issue without exploring it. Teachers then seize the opportunity to ask the core question but to credit the student for having the idea. The leader may begin, "Let's build on John's idea" and then ask the core question or say, "John, a moment ago, you said….Are you implying that… (fill in with core question or idea from preparation list)?" These are powerful chances to increase students' ownership for the direction of the seminar without their awareness that they are being manipulated into empowerment!

CLOSING QUESTIONS

Like the opening questions, only one of these is asked. Fittingly, it closes the seminar and has a unique purpose to connect some idea from the text to the life and experience of students. An absolute pattern emerging from recent studies of learning and the brain is that if emotion can be tapped, if connections with previous learning can be made, and relevance can be established, retention and learning increase. The sole purpose of the closing question is to create these personal links between content issues and the lives of students.

In the preceding example of "The Gettysburg Address," closing questions might be:

- "How do we currently view Lincoln's assertion that 'all men are created equal'?"
- "To what extent, in modern times, do we have government 'of the
  people, by the people, and for the people?'"
- "How have we responded to Lincoln's vision?"

In writing closing questions, leaders should keep several considerations in mind. Remember that this is the only question that may and, perhaps for the emphasis on personalization, *should* use the word "you" or "we." While the opening and core questions focus on textual understanding and implication, the closing clearly calls for leaving the text for a self-reference or modern application.

Another criterion when writing closing questions is to ensure that they are applicable to all students. For instance, a closing question about "The Gettysburg Address" may ask, "For what are you willing to give your 'last full measure of devotion?'" In other words, "What are you willing to die for?" This question makes an assumption on the teacher's part that all are willing to die for something. Students for whom this concept does not compute have nothing to say and are excluded unfairly from participation because of the teacher judgment embedded in the question.

Furthermore, the question violates another closing question imperative. While the question's purpose is to connect to the learner's life, it is not intended to pry or in any way force a student to reveal a vulnerability or a sensitivity. So, how do you strike a balance between a compelling question that touches some emotional chord and a relevance question that seems sterile and canned? How about these:

- "In our society, what are people willing to die for?"
- "Are high school students ever called upon to give 'the last full measure of devotion?'"

Might a student answer these closings with a personal revelation of what he would die for? Of course. But does the student also have the right to speculate about the actions of the group, teenagers, or our society? Of course. Now the question is still provocative without requiring the student's core to be exposed.

FOLLOWUP QUESTIONS

In an ideal seminar, the teacher asks the opening and never speaks again until the closing, as all cores are logically introduced and thoroughly explored by class members. However, students sometimes display faulty logic, do not defend their positions, hog the floor, or otherwise commit transgressions that require mild teacher intervention. Even Socrates did not find all his pupils' comments equally intriguing, and he examined their thinking, pushing or prodding them to clarify and defend their positions.

This is an important role of the seminar leader—to maintain a modicum of control over the direction and emphasis of seminar and to push for rigor where it is absent. A seminar is not a lovefest where everything said is equally significant. Comments are weighed and evaluated by the teacher, and under certain conditions, followup questions should be raised. Figure 6.1 illustrates moments that lend to followup questions.

FIGURE 6.1. FOLLOWUP QUESTIONS

Student Behavior	*Teacher Asks*
• Offers an opinion only	• "Where in the text do you find support for this point of view?"
• Uses a fuzzy, unclear explanation	• "What do you mean by…(repeats the fuzzy phrase)?"
• Gives a long explanation	• "Are you saying that…" (puts it in a nutshell)
• Heads down a wrong path	• "Would someone take issue with her point of view?" "What textural support is there for that position?"
• Engages in circular thinking, arriving nowhere	• "Can you make your point?"
• Makes a generalization	• "Why do you say that?"

These kinds of followup questions should be used sparingly so that the teacher's voice is only occasionally invoked. Too frequent a use of followups may either intimidate students or transfer ownership for seminar from students back to the teacher. Obviously, either condition is undesirable.

If teachers make clear their expectations that opinions on openings and cores should be defended with textual evidence and that students should think before speaking, the need for followups of this nature should become less frequent as students have more experience with the process. As students become more experienced participants, they begin to recognize the generalizations, circular thinking, faulty logic, or unsubstantiated opinions, and model the teacher behaviors, raising their hands to ask the appropriate followup questions themselves.

A real sense of empowerment occurs with students when they view seminar as their time, when their "teacher cannot interrupt," as one student saw it. The skilled seminar leader listens for discussion that touches a core issue and asks a question that "sounds like" a followup: "So are you saying that…(core issue)?"

A core question is on the table. The student gets the credit, and this seminar moment appears directed by the student.

The keen leader may also hear a student raise a question that is almost the same as a core. The teacher says, "Sounds like we have a new question" and then tweaks the student question to cover another core. Again, student ownership of seminar is preserved. A good leader listens for these opportunities to transfer ownership through the subtle manipulation of the wording of a question.

DEVELOPING SEMINAR QUESTIONS

Question development is critical to the success of the seminar. Before the seminar begins, the teacher must carefully process the information in the text, list all substantive ideas, issues, and quotations, anticipate students' reactions, and write thoughtful structured questions that will ensure that goals are achieved. Figure 6.2 (p. 68) offers guidelines for writing appropriate seminar questions.

(Text continues on page 69.)

FIGURE 6.2. GENERAL GUIDELINES FOR SOCRATIC QUESTIONING

♦ **Focus on the Goal**

The goal of the seminar is to enlarge understanding by exploring ideas and issues of text, not to establish facts.

♦ **Use Open-Ended Questions**

Avoid yes/no questions without followups. Ask no fact or single-answer questions.

♦ **Keep Questions Value-Free**

Participants make judgments, connections; teacher language remains neutral, free from ideas or a point of view.

♦ **Use Simple, Yet Provocative, Language**

Word choice is conversational and hits the mind, heart, or gut. Bury Bloom!

♦ **Use Questions with Meat**

Can the group explore this for 15–45 minutes? Does it prompt thinking beyond the obvious? It shouldn't be answerable without reading the text. Question arises from experiences, events, and language that are common to all.

♦ **Follow the Order of Question Types**

Use an opening question first, then three to eight core questions, and a closing question. Don't ask a listed question if it has already been answered.

♦ **Use Occasional Followup Questions**

Followup questions are not planned ahead, but are asked of individual speakers to clarify and probe. Examples include:

- "Are you saying that...?"
- "Where in the text do you find support for that?"
- "What do you mean by...?"
- "Would someone take issue with...?"
- "What is your point?"

These questions push the student to defend or clarify a view with proof and prompt others to challenge a view.

Once the teacher has selected a text and read it carefully, a two-step process occurs. First, the teacher should generate a listing of all important ideas that should be explored thoroughly or touched on during the seminar. Notice that the focus is on ideas embedded in or issues raised by the text, not on logical order, sequencing of events, character interactions, or finite details. This is rather a listing of big picture themes, overarching moments of clarity, passages or phrases that say it all or veil it all, episodes that mark the essence of the piece. These may be listed in no particular order. The purpose is merely to get them down as the raw material from which questions will be framed. Figure 6.3 (pp. 70–71) is an ideas sheet followed by a Socratic Seminar question sheet for organizing appropriate questions. Figure 6.4 (pp. 72–75) provides appropriate sample texts and questions for seminar.

It is somewhat dangerous to put canned (though good) questions in the hands of seminar leaders. For learning models of good questions that compel thought without giving judgment, for using student friendly language, and for distinguishing types of questions, placing questions in teachers' hands has value. However, there is no shortcut to preparation to lead a seminar.

Teachers should be thoroughly familiar with the text, list the essential ideas and issues, mark key passages, and have fine-tuned questions that draw those issues out. It is only this level of rereading and reflection, even if this is the third year the piece has been used, that will adequately have the teacher at a pitch to anticipate, to listen for students sniffing around an issue, to ask a key follow-up, and otherwise to manage the academic climate, among all the other management issues of leading a successful seminar.

Figure 6.3. TEACHER IDEA AND QUESTIONS SHEETS FOR SEMINAR PLANNING

Socratic Seminar on _____

I. Ideas, Issues, and Quotations that Should Be Explored

_____

_____

_____

_____

_____

_____

_____

_____

_____

_____

_____

_____

_____

_____

II. Socratic Questions

(1) OPENING QUESTIONS (Broad, directs into text, open-ended, provocative; *write 2, ask 1*)

1.

2.

(3–8) CORE QUESTIONS (Content specific, quotes, "how" or "why"; *write 3 to 8, ask what is necessary*)

1.

2.

3.

4.

5.

6.

7.

8.

(1) CLOSING QUESTION (Use "you," relevance, connection to real world or self; *write 2, ask 1*)

1.

2.

FIGURE 6.4. SAMPLE SEMINAR QUESTIONS

Text #1: *The Scarlet Letter* (Hawthorne) **English/Social Studies**

Opening   1. "A" traditionally stands for quality, excellence, the highest grade or the best performance. In *The Scarlet Letter,* why is the symbol "A" Hester's badge?

Core   1. What reactions does the "A" evoke?

                2. What kind of child is Pearl?

                3. What is Hester like as a mother?

                4. Are the characters taught anything by their experiences?

                5. Dimmesdale repeatedly says from the pulpit, "I am the worst of sinners." What does he mean?

                6. What is Hawthorne's portrayal of Chillingworth?

                7. From the time of the initial punishment, Hester is free to leave Boston. Why doesn't she?

Closing   1. Shaming type punishments, like the caning of the American in Singapore or an American judge in sentencing a man to wear the sign "I am a thief" while doing community service cleaning the sidewalk in front of the business he robbed, may be making a comeback. What do you think about public humiliation as a legal response to crime?

Text #2: "Mother to Son" (Langston Hughes) **Middle School/English/ Sociology**

Opening   1. The title "Mother to Son" suggests the mother has something to say to her son. What does she want him to know?

Core   1. What has life been like for the mother?

                2. What does the mother's language tell you about her?

                3. What does the mother mean by a "crystal stair"?

Closing   1. If you were a parent, what advice would you give your child?

2. What advice have adults in your life given you? (Note: Not "What advice did your mother give you?" because all have not been raised by a mother.)

3. What obstacles are on a teenager's "stair"?

Text #3: "The Earth Does Not Belong to Man; Man Belongs to the Earth" (Chief Seattle) **Social Studies/Environmental Science**

Opening   1. What message does Chief Seattle have for the "great chief" in Washington?

Core   1. Who is the "savage" here?

2. The chief says in line 30, "Our ways are different from your ways." In what ways are they different?

3. Several times the chief says, "All things are connected." What does he mean?

Closing   1. How has America answered Chief Seattle's prophecy?

2. What would Chief Seattle say about the land today?

3. Is Chief Seattle's wisdom relevant in our day and time?

Text # 4: "Lessons from Geese" (based on the work of Milton Olson) **Philosophy/Sociology**

Opening   1. What are the lessons from geese?

2. What connections are made between geese and people?

Core   1. Which lesson(s) contain the greatest truths?

2. Which lesson is most or least applicable to humans?

Closing   1. In our classroom (or "in our school" or "on our team") which lesson(s) do we most need to work on?

2. In our classroom, which lesson(s) do we do best?

Text # 5: "The Town Mouse and the Country Mouse" (Aesop's Fable)
Middle School/English

Opening   1. What's with these mice?

2. How do these mice view each other?

Core   1. What does the Town Mouse mean when he says, "I will show you how to live"?

2. What role does music play?

3. What do you make of the moral, "Better beans and bacon in peace than cakes and ale in fear"?

Closing   1. Here in Raleigh (or "in our school"), do we each make judgments about people based on where they are from?

Text #6: *Silent Spring* (Rachel Carson) **Science**

Opening   1. Rachel Carson references the work of Jean Rostard, who wrote, "The obligation to endure gives us the right to know." What do each of you now know as a result of reading Silent Spring? (Round robin after 3 minutes to reflect and scour the text.)

Core   1. Some teachers maintain that Silent Spring could be used as the biology text. How could this book be used to teach the units we have studied? (Table of contents for biology text is provided.)

2. What are the various alternatives, chemical and biological, suggested by Carson?

3. Carson has been accused of being a zealot, and a radical. What is your reaction to her views and presentation of information?

Closing   1. The book came out in 1962. Why are we reading it more than 35 years later?

2. What kind of citizen of the environment are we today (or will you be in 20 "springs")?

Text # 7: "Learn to Be Still" (Lyrics by The Eagles) **Middle School/English**

Opening	1. Why "learn to be still?"
	2. "It's waiting for you to awaken." What would The Eagles awaken in their audience?
Core	1. What do you make of the line, "We don't know how to be alone?"
	2. What are the "contradictions in all these messages we send" in lines 23 and 24?
	3. Why don't the "flowers smell so sweet"?
	4. After all the references to being still, why does the song end with "keep on runnin'"?
Closing	1. How does our culture view stillness?
	2. To what extent are we as a society (or a "community of 15-year-olds...") satisfied with our various stations in life?

Text # 8: "Law of Human Nature" (From *Mere Christianity* by C. S. Lewis) **Philosophy/Sociology**

Opening	1. According to Lewis, what is the law of human nature?
Core	1. What are the results or consequences of following or not following the laws of human nature?
	2. Is there any relationship between right and wrong and the laws of human nature? (Not "What is the relationship between right or wrong?" because that is teacher judgment. "Is there a relationship?" supposes there may or may not be one.)
	3. What indications are there of man's response when he breaks the laws?
Closing	1. How do you think future generations will interpret the law of human nature?
	2. For you, what is the most critical law of human nature?

7

LESSON DESIGN USING SEMINARS

Lesson design and planning units for the block schedule offer teachers new challenges as they strive to keep students interested, alert, and focused. Whether the class period is 80 minutes or 90 minutes, students must have a variety of activities that tap all learning styles and needs. Even adults have difficulty attending to a speaker for an extended period; consequently, no student should sit passively and listen to lecture for an entire period.

PLANNING IN THE BLOCK

Lesson planning traditionally has focused on one objective or one major topic with all activities revolving around it for 50 or 55 minutes. In the block schedule, however, teachers alternate between whole-period lesson plans and breaking the period into mini-lessons. The unit structure and needs of students dictate which lesson design is used. Before specifically addressing seminar lesson design, a review of sample time sequences, lesson designs, and a lesson plan log is in order. For someone already experienced in block scheduling, these models are familiar; however, for teachers just beginning block scheduling, planning for additional time is somewhat scary without models to consider.

Figure 7.1 gives sample time sequences for lessons in the block. These lesson sequences, which are applicable to all curricula areas, provide ideas about structuring time in the block with at least three activities in each class.

Adjusting planning to the block schedule is easier when teachers have several different formats to follow. While planning one focused 90-minute lesson is relatively straightforward, the three-part lesson design is somewhat more challenging for high school instructors. Middle school and elementary teachers have always planned mini-lessons to accommodate brief attention spans and shorter class periods, but most high school planning has been for the entire period. Figure 7.2 gives two different planning models.

FIGURE 7.1. SAMPLE 90-MINUTE TIME SEQUENCES

	Activity	Minutes
I.	1. Attendance, collecting homework, etc.	5
	2. Introduce new material; minilecture	20
	3. Activity	20
	4. Review or presentation	20
	5. Teacher-directed activity	15
	6. Homework assignment and closure	10
II.	1. Attendance, etc.	5
	2. Go over homework	15
	3. Reading-to-learn fact list	20
	4. Check for reading or for understanding—quiz	20
	5. Mini-lecture; notes	25
	6. Assignment and closure	5
III.	1. Writing activity	30
	a. Attendance	
	b. Check homework	
	2. Peer revision/editing	30
	3. Practice/second draft	25
	4 Closure	5
IV.	1. Preseminar task	15
	a. Attendance	
	b. Check for marking of text	
	2. Socratic seminar	60
	3. Postseminar task (response writing)	15
V.	1. Activity listed on board	10
	a. Attendance	
	b. Homework check or collection	
	2. Activity review	10
	3. Presentation of new material	30
	4. Group activity as followup	20
	5. Quiz	15
	6 Closure	5

**FIGURE 7.2. SAMPLE LESSON DESIGNS
FOR BLOCK SCHEDULING**

SAT Lesson Prep

(15 min.)	Mini-lecture: general information about taking the SAT.
(15 min.)	Strategies and whole group practice using strategies.
(15 min.)	Student practice and sharing of analogy sentences.
(30 min.)	Take practice verbal test.
(15 min.)	Sharing of answers and discussion of scoring; students determine their scores on the practice test.

Three-Part Lesson Design

Part I: 30-Minute Grammar Lesson: Correction of run-on sentences (use the overhead or blackboard)

(15 min.)	Give examples of run-on sentences. Model the five correction methods.
(5 min.)	Practice three to five sentences from textbook or handout.
(10 min.)	Put samples of corrected sentences on board and discuss.

Part II: 15-Minute Vocabulary Study

(15 min.)	Using the blackboard, list words, definitions, sample sentences. Discuss words and uses.

Part III: 45-Minute Literature Lesson: Discussion of short story which was read as homework

(10 min.)	Students complete a three-level study guide using text
(10 min.)	Group students and give each group an application question to discuss and present findings to the class.
(20 min.)	Groups present to class.
(5 min.)	Closure and homework.

Another planning aid is the lesson plan log. Although there are many styles of logs, the following model is an easy one to use in lesson planning for any subject. Using a log usually results in more detailed planning than is done with most lesson plan books. In the block schedule, students must have varied activities to get them actively involved. Figure 7.3 models a 90-minute lesson suitable for American literature or United States history. Figure 7.4 is a blank log that teachers can use to plan lessons, including those using seminar.

FIGURE 7.3. BLOCK LESSON PLAN LOG

Class_____ Date_____

Time: 90 minutes

(10 min.)

Introduce "protest" as a theme. Talk about protest movements in the 1960s.

(30 min.)

Play five protest songs. After each song, list on the board title, artist, time, cause, and artist's position on the issue.

(10 min.)

Make a list of conflicts, social conditions and causes in 1999 that individuals would want to protest.

(25 min.)

Group activity: Write a protest song.

(15 min.)

Share the song with the class. Talk about the group's position on the issue.

(____ min.) or homework:

Challenge musically gifted students to put the song to music or to perform for the class the next day.

Notes:

FIGURE 7.4. BLOCK LESSON PLAN LOG

Class_____   Date_____

Time: _____ minutes

_____

(____ min.)

Activity 1:

_____

(____ min.)

Activity 2:

_____

(____ min.)

Activity 3:

_____

(____ min.)

Activity 4:

_____

(____ min.)

Activity 5:

_____

(____ min.)

Homework:

_____

Notes:

PLANNING THE SOCRATIC SEMINAR

During the 90-minute periods, teachers may break the lesson into segments—group work, practice, mini-lecture, question and answer, or writing. On other occasions, however, the teacher uses the entire period for one activity, which frequently occurs when seminars are scheduled. The seminar lesson plan has three parts—preseminar, seminar, and postseminar. Time allotments for seminar vary depending on the length of the seminar text and on objectives and desired outcomes. All three activities can be completed in one day in class, or the preseminar can be done at home prior to seminar day. In addition, the postseminar can be finished as homework. Consider the time possibilities modeled in Figure 7.5 for scheduling the three components of seminar.

FIGURE 7.5. SUGGESTED SEMINAR TIME SEQUENCES

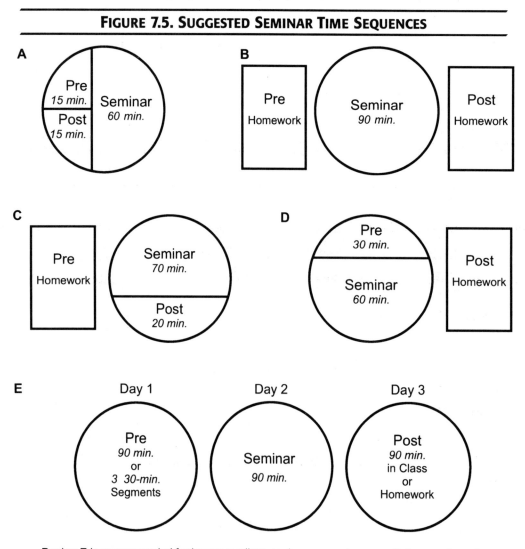

Design E is recommended for longer readings such as a novel or a nonfiction seminar piece.

Lesson design for seminar begins with determining unit and lesson objectives. Where does the seminar fit into the unit? Will the seminar introduce the unit, enrich a concept, integrate learning, establish relevance, or culminate the unit? Once these objectives have been established, the task is to select a seminar text (see Chapter 4). How long should the text be? How much time should be set aside in the plan for seminar?

PRESEMINAR PLANNING

Next, the teacher must develop preseminar tasks. The purpose of preseminar tasks is to prepare students for reading, to introduce the seminar text, and to check for reading readiness before beginning the seminar. Preseminar tasks can be reading activities and marking the text (see Chapter 3 for models) or other creative activities. The teacher decides whether preseminar tasks should be completed in class the day before seminar or on seminar day itself, or at home and presented on the day of seminar. Length and sophistication of the reading determine the preparation time. The degree of difficulty of the task is also a factor.

For example, teaching *The Scarlet Letter* through seminar is possible only with a class of strong readers. Even a strong class, however, must have ample preseminar preparation. Directed reading activities during the reading plus preseminar writing are useful. A typical preseminar task on *The Scarlet Letter* consists of several in-class essays done in conjunction with reading intervals. Suppose the class has been assigned the reading of chapters 1–8. On the day the reading is due, the teacher lists several thesis statements on the board that students should be knowledgeable about at this point in the reading. For 30 minutes, students write. After the second and third reading intervals, the process is repeated on different thesis statements. Meanwhile, feedback is given to students about ideas or issues they need to trace throughout the novel or to research in greater depth. For most gifted students, breaking down *The Scarlet Letter* into reading segments followed by writing is sufficient preparation for seminar.

Students, through their in-class writings, have received practice in documenting and supporting their positions on key issues. In addition, students have brainstormed and traced themes and characters throughout the text. By reviewing their writings the evening before seminar, they can prepare note sheets with page references for use during the seminar. Although the novel is lengthy, students who have completed assigned tasks should have little or no difficulty accessing quotations or page references as new ideas arise during the seminar.

How much time does the preseminar require? For the task just outlined, the teacher sets aside three 30-minute segments in the lesson plan over a period of 2 weeks prior to the seminar date. Remember, students are reading the novel and doing directed-reading activities outside of class. In class, other lessons are presented that require less homework and give the student time to read and prepare. When the entire preseminar is complete, the teacher has options—to count the three essays as 100 points for preseminar or to include the directed-reading activities as part of the preseminar grade. Teacher preference is the rule here; however, students must know that their preparatory work is valued.

Other preseminar tasks are more creative, especially when used in conjunction with another reading activity. In Chapter 3, suggestions were given for a directed reading on *All Quiet on the Western Front*, a relatively easy reading novel, often used in both English and social studies to explore the effects of war, to study character, and to understand the universality of war. Social studies classes often read the novel to culminate their study of World War I, to put human faces behind the weapons and bloodshed. Unlike *The Scarlet Letter*, students of all reading levels do remarkably well comprehending *All Quiet on the Western Front*, which makes it an ideal seminar text.

After students have finished their directed reading assignment, an innovative precursor to seminar is music—specifically, playing songs presenting varied views of war. As students listen to each song, they list the singer's attitudes toward war. After having heard all the songs, students then go to *All Quiet on the Western Front* and locate similar comments or contradicting views of war. Two reminders for teachers: First, list the titles and artists of songs on the board; second, don't allow students to discuss the music until the perception of war arises during seminar. Any prior discussion will water down the intensity of the seminar. The desire is to have students who are pumped for seminar after a lively, innovative preseminar task. Likely, the most appropriate time for presentation of this particular task is the day before seminar, because students need adequate time to trace references in the text.

Figure 7.6 is a reproducible preseminar task for *All Quiet on the Western Front*. The form can be easily modified for use with other texts where music is appropriate.

Other preseminar tasks are more generic and applicable to any text. For example, students may be asked to track changes of their opinions from before reading to after seminar. Rachel Carson's *Silent Spring* is a suitable text for this preseminar task. Before reading Carson's work, what are student attitudes on environmental issues and protection of the environment? After reading and seminar, which of their opinions are the same or changed? While the purpose of seminar is not to cause students to change their opinions, new information and the viewpoints of peers may have some influence on thinking.

As well, John Hersey's *Hiroshima* or an article on immigration in America could use the same preseminar task. Any time the teacher needs students to acknowledge and break down preconceived notions before moving into seminar, a listing of views before reading and changes in opinion after seminar is in order. For instance, Hersey asks the reader to experience the bombing from the survivors' perspective, a viewpoint radically different from the political perspective most students have heard repeatedly. To consider *Hiroshima* with an open mind free of bias, students need a preseminar task to establish direction.

FIGURE 7.6. PRESEMINAR TASK FOR
ALL QUIET ON THE WESTERN FRONT

1. _____Song Title   _____Artist

Viewpoint:

```


```

2. _____Song Title   _____Artist

Viewpoint:

```


```

3. _____Song Title   _____Artist

Viewpoint:

```


```

4. _____Song Title   _____Artist

Viewpoint:

```


```

5. _____Song Title   _____Artist

Viewpoint:

```


```

Figure 7.7 provides a chart that can be used for any text where opinions "before" and "after" have significance. Students may brainstorm individually on their views, or they may elect to gather ideas in small group discussions. To conclude, a think-pair-share exercise is an excellent way to share how views have changed. Actually, the listing of views prior to seminar is a preseminar activity, and the listing and sharing afterwards becomes a postseminar activity.

Another preseminar task traces character development, which is especially significant for selections with character foils or characters with complex actions and motivations. *Medea* and "Dr. Rappaccini's Daughter" are two texts that have intriguing and complex characters. As Jason and Medea struggle to end their marriage and Dr. Rappaccini and Dr. Baglioni conflict in their scientific ethics, keeping track of events, behaviors, and motivations is essential for understanding of character. Using a graphic organizer enables students to visually track characters. While many styles of organizers are available, a simple design is best for a preseminar task, especially if the task is done in class prior to the seminar. Also, to trace opposing characters, students need parallel organizers with the two character foils side by side. If other characters besides the main ones are influential, they may also be followed as part of the preseminar assignment. If the seminar followup assignment is a writing dealing with character, the preseminar is a good place for students to brainstorm and prewrite using an organizer. Figure 7.8 (pp. 88–89) is a reproducible graphic organizer that can be used to trace character.

For a nonfiction text, identifying the positions of individuals or groups on important issues is necessary. Consider the cloning debate. One must entertain views from the populace, politicians, scientists, legal experts, and the religious and medical community. As a preseminar task, students should look carefully at all these perspectives before discussing articles on the ethical nature of cloning. Figure 7.9 (p. 90) provides an organizer for this task.

Preseminar tasks can vary in length and depth. Whenever possible, teachers should design tasks that satisfy existing class requirements. Preseminar should not be an add-on activity but one that better prepares students in reading, critical thinking, and accessing of information. Figure 7.10 (p. 91) gives samples of short preseminar tasks that can be completed in class prior to seminar.

(Text continues on page 91.)

FIGURE 7.7 TRACKING VIEWPOINTS
BEFORE AND AFTER SEMINAR

Seminar Title _____   Date _____

Views & Opinions

Before Reading	*After Reading & Seminar*	*Changes*

FIGURE 7.8. PRESEMINAR ORGANIZER FOR
CHARACTER DEVELOPMENT

Circle: list character's name.
Line: identify action or event
Block: explain result or motivation

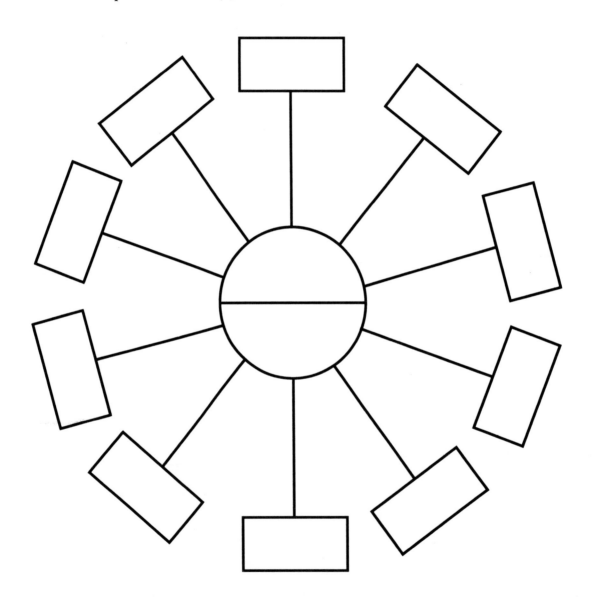

Use to track character foils.

Circle: list character's name.
Line: identify action or event
Block: explain result or motivation

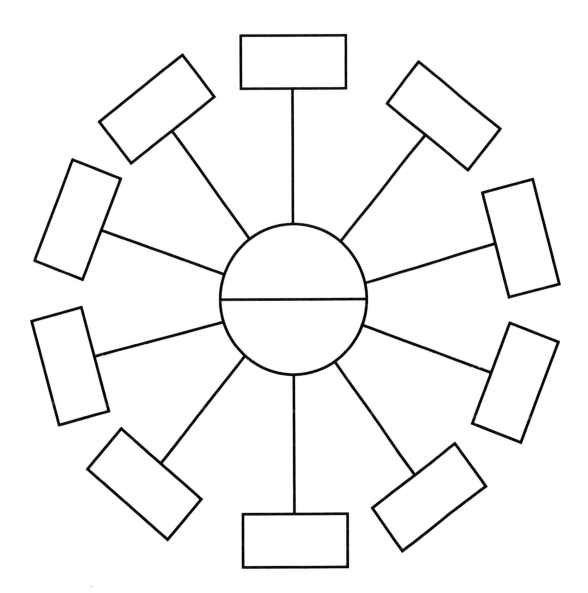

Use to track character foils.

FIGURE 7.9. PRESEMINAR POSITION ON ISSUES CHART

Issue: *Group or Character*   *Position*

1)

2)

3)

4)

5)

6)

7)

8)

9)

10)

Notes:

FIGURE 7.10. SAMPLE PRESEMINAR TASKS

- Complete a reading comprehension quiz or test.

- Complete a directed reading task or questions.

- Write a reflective sentence that states the focus of the text or of chapters in a novel.

- List at least ten major issues that should be covered in seminar.

- Mark the text and/or prepare a notesheet with page numbers for referencing the text.

- Freewrite on the selection for 15 minutes prior to seminar.

- Use graphic organizers to trace main ideas or character development.

- Use graphic organizers to compare and contrast the development in two characters.

- Use an organizer to track your opinion on key issues before the seminar and changes in opinion afterwards.

- Prepare a list of questions you want answered in seminar.

POSTSEMINAR PLANNING

A postseminar assignment enriches and extends the learning, and thus maximizes all the foregoing efforts of students and teachers. Postseminar assignments can be brief enough to complete in class, or more extensive, requiring additional reading, research, or writing. Teachers should use the postseminar activity to increase learning and to satisfy curricular objectives.

For example, a seminar on *The Scarlet Letter* may be extended through several activities. Because the novel is rich in themes and implications for modern society, students may be assigned formal essays as a followup task. Another creative activity is writing and presenting dramatic monologues as characters from the novel. This is an exciting way for students to demonstrate their understanding of character. Figure 7.11 (p. 92) presents a dramatic monologue design, and Figure 7.12 (p. 93) is an assessment instrument for the monologue. Figure 7.13 (p. 94) can be used for the presentation of the monologue.

While assessment is not the focus here, models are included for these seminar components as each part is introduced in an effort to show the overall range of seminars. Besides, teachers are usually more willing to incorporate new strategies into their lesson design if they have useable models to get them started. Because the seminar discussion is the most exciting part of the process, sometimes preseminar and postseminar tasks are dispensed with, which is not advisable. All three components are needed in the lesson design.

(Text continues on page 95.)

**FIGURE 7.11. *THE SCARLET LETTER* TASK DESIGN
FOR DRAMATIC MONOLOGUE FOR POSTSEMINAR**

- General Information:

  A dramatic monologue is a poetic form that presents a single character speaking. A monologue has these characteristics:

  - A single person is speaking at a critical time.

  - This person is addressing one or more other people. A dramatic monologue is somewhat like overhearing one end of a telephone conversation, but we know of the auditors' presence, who they are, and what they say or do only by the clues in the discourse of the single speaker.

  - The monologue is contrived so that the main focus is on the interesting temperament or character revealed by the dramatic speaker.

- Suggested Prewriting Activities:

  - Make lists of characters and their traits and motivations.

  - Free write on critical scenes from the novel.

- Suggested Writing Focuses:

  - All monologues should consist of multiple paragraphs.

  - When the monologue is delivered orally in class, it should last from 3 to 5 minutes.

  - The introduction must grab the reader/listener and pull him into the character's situation.

  - The body must explore the character's situation in depth, his emotions, his troubles, his motives, and relationships.

  - The conclusion should surprise the reader in some way by revealing something unexpected or tantalizing.

- Format:

  - Normal paragraphs with five-space indentation.

FIGURE 7.12. DRAMATIC MONOLOGUE EVALUATION INSTRUMENT

____ 1. Prewriting (10 Points)
   a. Freewriting
   b. Listing or graphic organizer

____ 2. Audience/Purpose (observation) (10)

____ 3. Tone (10)
   a. Diction
   b. Empathy with character

____ 4. Organization (Development/Detail) (25)
   a. Lead/Hook
      1. Interests reader
      2. Sustainable focus
   b. Body
      1. Sufficiently elaborated
      2. Multiple paragraphs
   c. Conclusion: surprising or intriguing point

____ 5. Sentence/Word Choice Sophistication (10)
   a. Sentence variety/style
   b. Varied sentence beginnings
   c. Strong verbs (avoidance of linking verbs)
   d. Carefully chosen words (power words)

____ 6. Format—paragraphs (5)

____ 7. Drafting/Revising (20)
   a. At least three drafts
   b. Substantive changes on one draft
   c. After second draft—use of revision checklist as indicator of change

____ 8. Editing (10)
   a. Evidence of editing changes on next to last draft
   b. Signature of proofreader on next to last draft (self, parent, peer)

Figure 7.13. *The Scarlet Letter* Dramatic Monologue: Presentation Evaluation for Postseminar

Presentation Design

A dramatic monologue is an interpretative portrayal of a single character. The presenter must grab the listeners' attention and make him connect emotionally with the character. For the dramatic presentation to be effective, the presenter must *become the character,* speaking with the character's voice and persona. Content of monologue has previously been assessed by another rubric. Assessment of presentation deals only with in-class portrayal of the character.

Presentation Assessment

Evaluation Checklist: Rate 1–5, with 5 as the highest score. Each category is worth 10 points.

_____ 1. Captures the character's personality

_____ 2. Grabs the listener's attention and pulls him into the character's situation.

_____ 3. Shows emotions and passion when appropriate

_____ 4. Surprises the reader by revelation or presentational approach

_____ 5. Speaks from three to five minutes.

_____ 6. Presents without notes—has memorized the monologue

_____ 7. Establishes eye contact and stage presence with the audience

_____ 8. Uses gestures suitable to scene and character

_____ 9. Speaks with appropriate rate and volume

_____ 10. Dresses to enhance character portrayal

A third way to enrich *The Scarlet Letter* seminar is to assign additional writing of current news articles that relate to the novel: "Paying for Crime with Shame" from *USA Today*, June 12, 1997; "The Name of the Game is Shame" from *Newsweek*, Dec. 12, 1994; and "Cheating Hearts, Mixed Feelings" from *USA Today*, June 12, 1997. As students read about American attitudes toward adultery and use of shaming as a deterrent against crime, they will understand how society still struggles with the same issues Hawthorne explored in 1850. Now students can discuss the articles in small groups or write position essays or reactions to the legacy of *The Scarlet Letter*. (If students cannot master the novel for seminar, the articles are an excellent text for seminar.)

Other postseminar assignments can be creative or artistic. For example, an ideal task to extend the *All Quiet on the Western Front* seminar is to have students rewrite scenes. Because the novel is narrated by Paul, a young German soldier who was the United States' enemy in World War I, students might retell the events as a French or American soldier. What is fascinating is how students have forgotten Paul's nationality. They sympathize and commiserate with him, wanting him to survive. Rewriting the scene evokes a myriad of emotions as the United States' role in the war is defined. Students especially enjoy this task if they have freedom to combine events from several scenes for dramatic effect.

An artistic approach to postseminar can be achieved through cartooning or other drawings. Two examples spring to mind. Creating a class "Wall of Remembrance" is a fitting tribute to Elie Wiesel's *Night* as students design their individual artistic tribute to the Holocaust victims and hang theirs along side those of their peers. Reading and discussing the Holocaust is gut-wrenching for many students, so their art is something of a catharsis as they respond to Wiesel's plea for the world to "never forget."

Cartooning is also a creative postseminar task. To conclude "How Much Land Does a Man Need," students have fun capturing Tolstoy's moral—that materialistic possessions are worth nothing at death—in cartoons depicting current popular culture. Allowing students to complete creative postseminar tasks showcases unique talents that are sometimes neglected.

Figure 7.14 (p. 96) lists some postseminar tasks that enrich and extend the seminar learning.

Before receiving any preseminar and postseminar assignments, students benefit from having design and assessment instruments that outline teacher expectations. When students know what is expected from them, they invariably improve their performance. The model lessons beginning on page 100 consist of preseminar and postseminar design instruments, time sequences, and seminar questions. Because the focus of this chapter is lesson design, all assessment instruments for the model lessons can be found in Chapter 9.

Figure 7.15 (p. 98) is a form that teachers can use in preparation of seminar lessons. Creating preseminar and postseminar design is much easier if this form is completed first.

FIGURE 7.14. SAMPLE POSTSEMINAR TASKS

- Write a composition on a particular topic that was addressed in seminar.
- Write a response essay that evaluates or clarifies points made or not made during the seminar.
- Follow the seminar with a research project.
- Read another work that has similarity or contrast. Write an essay exploring both.
- Respond in writing to a closing question or to another issue which was not discussed thoroughly.
- Do creative writing, art, or cartooning.
- Write a rebuttal to the seminar text.
- Participate in a think-pair-share activity.
- Be a participant in a panel discussion.
- Depending on the topic, write a letter that calls for action on a specific issue.
- Write a letter to a character in the work.

*This page has been intentionally left blank to allow
Figure 7.15 to be printed on facing pages.*

FIGURE 7.15. TEACHER WORKSHEET FOR SEMINAR LESSON DESIGN

Unit: _____

Seminar Text: _____   Length of Text: _____

Lesson Objectives:	*Main Points for Seminar:*

Seminar Time Allowance: _____ Point Value of Seminar: _____

Desired Outcomes:

Seminar Questions:

Opening Questions:

Core Questions:

Closing Questions:

Preseminar:

Task Description: _____

Format: _____ Length: _____

Point Value: _____

Postseminar:

Task Description: _____

Format: _____ Length: _____

Point Value: _____

MODEL LESSON PLANS

MODEL LESSON 1: "THIS SACRED SOIL"

Yonder sky that has wept tears of compassion upon my people for centuries untold and which to us appears changeless and eternal, may change. Today is fair. Tomorrow it may be overcast with clouds. My words are like the stars that never change. Whatever Seattle says the great chief at Washington can rely upon with as much certainty as he can upon the return of the sun or the seasons.

The White Chief says that Big Chief at Washington sends us greetings of friendship and goodwill. That is kind of him for we know he has little need of our friendship in return. His people are many. They are like the grass that covers vast prairies. My people are few. They resemble the scattering trees of a storm-swept plain....I will not dwell on, nor mourn over, our untimely decay, nor *reproach* our pale face brothers with hastening it, as we too may have been somewhat to blame....

Your God is not our God. Your God loves your people and hates mine. He folds his strong and protecting arms lovingly about the paleface and leads him by the hand as a father leads his infant son—but He has forsaken His red children—if they really are his. Our God, the Great Spirit, seems also to have forsaken us. Your God makes your people strong every day. Soon they will fill the land. Our people are ebbing away like a rapidly receding tide that will never return. The white man's God cannot love our people or He would protect them. They seem to be orphans who can look nowhere for help. How then can we be brothers?...We are two distinct races with separate origins and separate destinies. There is little in common between us.

To us the ashes of our ancestors are sacred and their resting place is hallowed ground. You wander far from the graves of your ancestors and seemingly without regret. Your religion was written upon tables of stone by the iron finger of your God so that you could not forget. The Red Man could never comprehend nor remember it. Our religion is the traditions of our ancestors—the dreams of our old men, given them in solemn hours of night by the Great Spirit; and the visions of our *sachems*; and it is written in the hearts of our people.

Your dead cease to love you and the land of their nativity as soon as they pass the portals of the tomb and wander way beyond the stars. They are soon forgotten and never return. Our dead never forget the beautiful world that gave them being.

Day and night cannot dwell together. The Red Man has ever fled the approach of the White Man, as the morning mist flees before the morning sun. However, your proposition seems fair and I think that my people will accept it and will retire to the reservation you offer them. Then we will dwell apart in peace....It matters little where we pass the remnant of our days. They will not be many. A few more moons; a few more winters—and not one of the descendants of the mighty hosts that once moved over this broad land or lived in happy homes, protected by the Great Spirit, will remain to mourn over the graves of a people once more powerful and hopeful than yours. But why should

I mourn at the untimely fate of my people? Tribe follows tribe, and nation follow nation, like the waves of the sea. It is the order of nature, and regret is useless. Your time of decay may be distant, but it will surely come, for even the White Man whose God walked and talked with him as friend with friend, cannot be exempt from the common destiny. We may be brothers after all. We will see.

Every part of this soil is sacred in the estimation of my people. Every hillside, every valley, every plain and grove, has been hallowed by some sad or happy event in days long vanished. The very dust upon which you now stand responds more lovingly to their footsteps than to yours, because it is rich with the blood of our ancestors and bare feet are conscious of the sympathetic touch. Even the little children who lived here and rejoiced here for a brief season will love these somber solitudes and at eventide they greet shadowy returning spirits. And when the last Red Man shall have perished, and the memory of my tribe shall have become a myth among the White Men, these shores will swarm with the invisible dead of my tribe, and when your children's children think themselves alone in the field, the store, the shop, upon the highway, or in the silence of the pathless woods, they will not be alone. At night when the streets of your cities and villages are silent and you think them deserted, they will throng with the returning hosts that once filled and still love this beautiful land. The White Man will never be alone.

Let him be just and deal kindly with my people, for the dead are not powerless. Dead, did I say? There is no death, only a change of worlds.

FIGURE 7.16. TEACHER WORKSHEET FOR SEMINAR "THIS SACRED SOIL"

Unit: English—"Native American Influences on American Literature
       Social Studies—"Clash of Cultures"
       Science—"Reservation of Nature"
       Sociology—"Identity"

Seminar Text: "This Sacred Soil"   Length of Text: 1 page

Lesson Objectives:	*Main Points for Seminar:*
• To identify conflict	• Causes of conflict
• To compare the white man and Indian way of life	• Views of God and the earth
• To discuss opposing views of the earth and nature	• Respect for the death
• To understand Native American beliefs and practices	• Religion
• To identify foreshadowing	• End of a culture
	• Brotherhood
	• Common destiny
	• Prophecy for the future

Seminar Time Allowance: 40 min   Point Value of Seminar: 50 pts

Desired Outcomes: Increased understanding of Native Americans'
    values

Seminar Questions:

Opening Question: What message does Chief Seattle have for the
    Big Chief at Washington?

Core Question: In paragraph 2, Chief Seattle says, "I will not
    dwell on, nor mourn over, our untimely decay, nor re-
    proach our pale face brothers with hastening it, as we too
    may have been somewhat to blame...." Does he do any of
    these things?

Closing Question: What personal messages can a 1990s teen
draw from "This Sacred Soil"?

Preseminar:

Task Description: Describe portrayals of Native Americans in movies,
television shows, and literature.

Format: Informal essay   Length: 1½ to 2 pages

Point Value: 30 points of seminar grade

Postseminar:

Task Description: If Native American beliefs and practices were applied
to today's society, what would be the effect?

Format: Response writing   Length: 1 or more pages

Point Value: 20 points of seminar score

FIGURE 7.17. TASK DESIGN FOR PRESEMINAR ON "THIS SACRED SOIL"

General Information:

A preseminar task is one component of the seminar process. This task, whatever it may be, is intended to cause the student to think deeply about the seminar selection before the discussion begins. The task also allows the facilitator to assess the student's reading readiness by concentrating on information the student should possess if he or she is prepared for seminar.

Suggested Preparation Activities:

1. As you read, mark your text for main ideas and interesting facts.
2. Keep a notesheet where you trace significant ideas through the selection.
3. Include page numbers for referencing the text.
4. Identify issues or questions you want to explore in the text.

Task:

1. Select three films, television shows, or pieces of literature that have Native American characters.
2. Describe three portrayals of Native Americans in these works. Focus on whether the portrayals are positive or negative. Identify stereotypical images.
3. The form of the writing is an informal essay—one draft in class. It must have an introduction, body, and conclusion.
4. The essay must be at least three or more paragraphs and 1½ to 2 pages.
5. Write in first person point of view.
6. Draft the essay in blue or black ink.

Assessment:

1. The preseminar task is worth 30 points of the seminar grade.
2. All elements of composition will be assessed: paragraphing, thesis, topic sentences, and elaboration.
3. Punctuation, spelling, usage, and sentence structure will be evaluated.
4. *Major focus* will be content and your understanding of literary and film portrayals of Native Americans.

FIGURE 7.18. POSTSEMINAR TASK DESIGN
ON "THIS SACRED SOIL"

General Information:

A postseminar task is the final component of the seminar process. This task is designed to showcase what the participant has learned from reading, discussing, and analyzing the text. The length of the task and the point value of the task may vary.

Suggested Preparation Activities:

1. Review the notes you took during seminar.
2. Think about what each contributor said and the reasons for his or her position on the issues.
3. Think about issues that received superficial coverage in the seminar.

Task:

1. Write a response essay reflecting on this question: If Native American beliefs and practices were applied to modern society, what would be the effect?
2. The format of writing should be an extended paragraph.
3. Prewrite before you begin the draft.
4. Formulate a strong topic sentence that states the position.
5. Give 3 supporting statements and elaboration of each point.
6. Conclude with a clincher sentence that pulls the response together and gives it a sense of finality.
7. Write in third person point of view.
8. Draft essay in blue or black ink.

Assessment:

1. The postseminar task is worth 20 points of the total seminar grade.
2. All elements of composition writing will be assessed.
3. Accuracy in grammar, spelling, usage, punctuation, and sentence structure are essential.
4. *Major focus* will be your ability to answer the question logically, based on Chief Seattle's teachings. Refer to the text for supporting details.
5. The writer must use the time in class for prewriting; however, the draft may be finished as homework.

MODEL LESSON 2: "THE FROGS DESIRING A KING"

The Frogs were living as happy as could be in a marshy swamp that suited them; they went splashing about caring for nobody and nobody troubling with them. But some of them thought that this was not right, that they should have a king and a proper constitution, so they determined to send up a petition to Jove to give them what they wanted. "Mighty Jove," they cried, "send unto us a king that will rule over us and keep us in order." Jove laughed at their croaking and threw down into the swamp a huge Log, which came down—kersplash—into the swamp. The Frogs were frightened out of their lives by the commotion made in their midst, and all rushed to the bank to look at the horrible monster; but after a time, seeing that it did not move, one or two of the boldest of them ventured out towards the Log, and even dared to touch it; still it did not move. Then the greatest hero of the Frogs jumped unto the Log and commenced dancing up and down upon it. There upon all the Frogs came and did the same; and for some time the Frogs went about their business every day without taking the slightest notice of their new King Log lying in their midst. But this did not suit them, so they sent another petition to Jove, and said to him, "We want a real king; one that will really rule over us." Now this made Jove angry, so he sent among them a big Stork that soon set to work gobbing them all up. Then the Frogs repented when too late.

"Better No Rule Than Cruel Rule."

FIGURE 7.19. TEACHER WORKSHEET FOR SEMINAR ON "THE FROGS DESIRING A KING"

Unit: Social Studies—"Revolution As a Tool for Change"
Seminar Text: Aesop's Fable, "The Frogs Desiring a King"
Length of Text: 1 page

Lesson Objectives:	*Main Points for Seminar:*
• To introduce revolution as a tool for political change	• Life the frogs live without a king
• To evaluate whether a central leader is good or bad	• Their need for a ruler
• To explore what makes a good leader	• Their reactions to the log
• To explore why humans need leaders	• Jove's response
• To consider the citizenry's role in government	• End results
	• Life lessons
	• How humans and frogs are alike

Seminar Time Allowance: 30 min   Point Value of Seminar: 40 pts

Desired Outcomes: That students will make the transfer that the experience of the frogs is not unlike human experience with revolution; that students will consider whether getting their wishes is always the best thing

Seminar Questions:

Opening Question: How is life for the frogs?

Core Question: Why do the frogs want a king?

Closing Question: What can civilizations learn from the frogs' experience?

Preseminar:

Task Description: To complete an argument chart prior to reading the fable, responding to this statement: Everyone needs a strong ruler.

Format: Graphic organizer

Time: 20 minutes in class (15 minutes for organizer and 5 minutes to read)

Point Value: 20 points of seminar grade

Postseminar:

Task Description: Using the preseminar graphic organizer as prewriting, write an essay arguing the point: "Everyone needs a strong leader."

Time in class: 30 minutes—complete final draft at home

Format: Position essay   Length: 2 or more pages

Point Value: 40 points of seminar score

FIGURE 7.20. PRESEMINAR TASK DESIGN ON "THE FROGS DESIRING A KING"

Task:

1. Before reading the fable, complete an argument chart in response to this question: "Everyone needs a strong leader."
2. You have 15 minutes to finish the chart and 5 minutes to read the one page seminar text.
3. The organizer is the prewriting for the postseminar assignment.
4. Write in complete sentences.
5. Total point value of preseminar is 20 points of total seminar grade.

Statement:

Supporting information: Think about the benefits and drawbacks of a leader.

Pros:

Cons:

Conclusion:

FIGURE 7.21. POSTSEMINAR TASK DESIGN ON "THE FROGS DESIRING A KING"

General Information:

A postseminar task is the final component of the seminar process. This task is designed to showcase what the participant has learned from reading, discussing, and analyzing the text. The length of the task and the point value of the task may vary.

Suggested Preparation Activities:

1. Review the notes you took during seminar.
2. Think about what each contributor said and the reasons for his or her position on the issues.
3. Think about issues that received superficial coverage in the seminar.

Task:

1. Using the preseminar graphic organizer as prewriting, write a position essay arguing the statement: "Everyone needs strong leaders."
2. Write a two draft essay of four or five paragraphs.
   a. The introduction should hook the reader and state the writer's position.
   b. Each body paragraph should argue either the benefits or detriments of a strong leader in support of the thesis statement.
   c. The conclusion should briefly restate the essential argument and give the essay a sense of finality.
3. Purpose: to argue a point; to take a position.
4. Point of view: third person.
5. Tone: serious.
6. Drafting: two drafts with the final in blue or black ink or typed.
7. Length: a minimum of two pages.
8. Time: 30 minutes in class—complete final draft for homework.

Assessment:

1. The postseminar task is worth 40 points of the total seminar grade.
2. All elements of composition writing will be assessed.
3. Accuracy in grammar, spelling, usage, punctuation, and sentence structure are essential.
4. *Major focus* will be strength of argument, originality of thinking, and mastery of writing skills.

MODEL LESSON 3: "A PSALM OF LIFE"

Tell me not, in mournful members,
Life is but an empty dream!—
For the soul is dead that slumbers.
And things are not what they seem.

Life is real! Life is earnest!
And the grave is not its goal:
Dust thou art, to dust returnest.
Was not spoken of the soul.

Not enjoyment, and not sorrow.
Is our destined end or way;
But to act, that each tomorrow
Find us farther than today.

Art is long, and Time is fleeting.
And, our hearts, though stout and brave.
Still, like muffled drums, are beating
Funeral marches to the grave.

In the world's broad field of battle,
In the bivouac of Life,
Be not like dumb, driven cattle!
Be a hero in the strife!

Trust no Future, howe'er pleasant!
Let the dead Past bury its dead!
Act—act in the living Present!
Heart within, and God o'erhead!

Lives of great men all remind us
We can make our lives sublime.
And, departing, leave behind us
Footprints on the sands of time;

Footprints, that perhaps another,
Sailing o'er life's solemn main.
A forlorn and shipwrecked brother,
Seeing, shall take heart again.

Let us, then, be up and doing.
With a heart for any fate;
Still achieving, still pursuing,
Learn to labor and to wait.

**FIGURE 7.22. TEACHER WORKSHEET FOR SEMINAR:
LONGFELLOW'S "A PSALM OF LIFE"**

Unit: English—"Early American Poetry—the Fireside Poets"

Seminar Text: Longfellow's "A Psalm of Life"

Length of Text: 1 page

Lesson Objectives:	*Main Points for Seminar:*
• To introduce Longfellow, one of the five major poets	• To extract themes
• To see the poet's philosophy of life	• To discuss Longfellow's message
• To discuss a psalm	• To discuss the sense of urgency in the poem
• To evaluate the style of the poem	• To consider implications of the poem and the value of life
• To read other Longfellow poems for comparison and contrast	• To see imperatives

Seminar Time Allowance: 40 min   Point Value of Seminar: 40 pts

---

Desired Outcomes: That students will gain a greater understanding of the quality of life and their need to give something back instead of always taking

---

Seminar Questions:

Opening Question: What does Longfellow know about life?

Core Questions: What does he mean when he says, "for the soul is dead that slumbers"?

Why are our "hearts beating funeral marches to the grave"?

What does he say people should not be?

What are the "footprints on the sands of time"?

Closing Question: Longfellow says, "Let us, then, be up and doing....Still achieving, still pursuing...." What should you personally be up, doing, achieving, and pursuing?

Preseminar:

Task Description: To find a song by a modern artist that expresses in some way your philosophy of life.

Format: Bring lyrics to class; paired sharing; prepare poster with song's theme

Time: 30 minutes in class (20 minutes for sharing and poster and 10 minutes to read "A Psalm of Life")

Point Value: 20 points of seminar grade

Postseminar:

Task Description: Write an original poem that expresses your attitudes and aspirations for life.

Time in class: 20 minutes—complete final draft at home

Format: Lyric poem   Length: 3 or more stanzas

Point Value: 40 points of seminar score

FIGURE 7.23. PRESEMINAR TASK DESIGN ON "A PSALM OF LIFE"

General Information:

A preseminar task is one component of the seminar process. This task, whatever it may be, is intended to cause the student to think deeply about the seminar selection before the discussion begins. The task also allows the facilitator to assess the student's reading readiness by concentrating on information the student should possess if he or she is prepared for seminar.

Suggested Preparation Activities:

1. As you read, mark your text for main ideas and interesting facts.
2. Keep a note sheet where you trace significant ideas through the selection.
3. Include page numbers for referencing the text.
4. Identify issues or questions you want to explore in the text.

Task:

1. Find a song by a modern artist that expresses in part your philosophy of life.
2. Copy the lyrics, to be submitted, and bring them to class.
3. In class, pair with another student and read each other's lyrics.
4. Briefly discuss what the song means to each of you.
5. Create a poster with the title, artist, and message of the songs listed.
6. Hang on the wall for the class to view.
7. Time: 30 Minutes (20 minutes to discuss and prepare poster; 10 minutes to read "A Psalm of Life")

Assessment:

1. The preseminar task is worth 20 points of the seminar grade.
2. *Major focus* will be completion of the assignment and time on task in the paired activity.

FIGURE 7.24. POSTSEMINAR TASK DESIGN
ON "A PSALM OF LIFE"

General Information:

A postseminar task is the final component of the seminar process. This task is designed to showcase what the participant has learned from reading, discussing, and analyzing the text. The length of the task and the point value of the task may vary.

Suggested Preparation Activities:

1. Review the notes you took during seminar.
2. Think about what each contributor said and the reasons for his or her position on the issues.
3. Think about issues that received superficial coverage in the seminar.

Task:

1. Write an original poem that expresses your attitudes and aspirations for life.
2. Format: lyric poem that evokes a strong emotion.
3. Length: 3 or more stanzas.
4. Drafting: 2 drafts with the final draft done in blue or black ink or typed.
5. Time: 20 minutes to write in class; final draft to be completed as homework.

Assessment:

1. The postseminar task is worth 40 points of the total seminar grade.
2. Accuracy in grammar, spelling, usage, punctuation, and line structure are essential.
3. Rhyming is not necessary!
4. *Major focus* will be your content and the effective presentation of your attitudes and aspirations for life.

MODEL LESSON 4: "SELF-RELIANCE"

There is a time in every man's education when he arrives at the conviction that envy is ignorance; that imitation is suicide; that he must take himself for better, for worse, as his portion; that though the wide universe is full of good, no kernel of nourishing corn can come to him but through his toil bestowed on that plot of ground which is given to him to till. The power which resides in him is new in nature, and none but he knows what that is which he can do, nor does he know until he has tried. Not for nothing one face, one character, one fact makes much impression on him, and another none. It is not without preestablished harmony, this sculpture in the memory. The eye was placed where one ray should fall that it might testify of that particular ray. Bravely let him speak the utmost syllable of his confession. We but half express ourselves, and are ashamed of that divine idea which each of us represents. It may be safely trusted as proportionate and of good issues, so it be faithfully imparted, but God will not have his work made manifest by cowards. It needs a divine man to exhibit anything divine. A man is relieved and gay when he has put his heart into his work and done his best; but what he has said or done otherwise, shall give him no peace. It is a deliverance which does not deliver. In the attempt his genius deserts him; no muse befriends; no invention, no hope.

Trust thyself: every heart vibrates to that iron string. Accept the place the divine Providence has found for you; the society of your contemporaries, the connection of events. Great men have always done so and confided themselves childlike to the genius of their age, betraying their perception that the Eternal was stirring at their heart, working through their hands, predominating in all their being. And we are now men, and must accept in the highest mind the same transcendent destiny; and not pinched in a corner, not cowards fleeing before a revolution, but redeemers and benefactors, pious aspirants to be noble clay plastic under the Almighty effort, let us advance and advance on Chaos and the Dark....

These are the voices which we hear in solitude, but they grow faint and inaudible as we enter into the world. Society everywhere is in conspiracy against the manhood of every one of its members. Society is a joint-stock company in which the members agree for the better securing of his bread to each shareholder, to surrender the liberty and culture of the eater. The virtue in most request is conformity. Self-reliance is its aversion. It loves not realities and creators, but names and customs.

Whoso would be a man must be a nonconformist. He who would gather immortal palms must not be hindered by the name of goodness, but must explore if it be goodness. Nothing is at last sacred but the integrity of our mind. Absolve you to yourself, and you shall have the suffrage of the world....

A foolish consistency is the hobgoblin of little minds, adored by little statesmen and philosophers and divines. With consistency a great soul has simply nothing to do. He may as well concern himself with his shadow on the wall. Out upon your guarded lips! Sew them up with packthread, do. Else, if you would be a man, speak what you think today in words as hard as cannon balls, and tomorrow speak what tomorrow thinks in hard words again though it contradicts everything you said today. Ah, then, exclaim the aged ladies, you shall be sure to be misunderstood. Misunderstood! It is a right fool's word. Is it so bad then to be misunderstood? Pythagoras was misunderstood, and Socrates, and Jesus, and Luther, and Copernicus, and Galileo, and Newton, and every pure and wise spirit that ever took flesh. To be great is to be misunderstood.

**FIGURE 7.25. TEACHER WORKSHEET FOR SEMINAR
ON "SELF-RELIANCE"**

Unit: English—"Voices in American Literature"

Seminar Text: Ralph Waldo Emerson's "Self-Reliance," 1841

Length of Text: 1 page

Lesson Objectives:	*Main Points for Seminar:*
• To introduce Emerson as one of the key voices of the mid 1800s	• Imitation as a lifestyle
• To emphasize conformity vs. nonconformity	• Integrity
	• Trust in self
• To discuss characteristics of individualism	• Society
	• Self-reliance
• To consider contributions of people Emerson admired	• Ability to change one's mind
	• Great men and why
• To understand function of society	• Nonconformist

Seminar Time Allowance: 70 min   Point Value of Seminar: 75 pts

Suggestion: Play audio recording of "Self-Reliance" before starting seminar.

> Desired Outcomes: Students will grasp what Emerson means by
> *self-reliance*; students will discuss society's attempt to shape
> the individual; students will define what individualism means
> in their own lives

Seminar Questions:

Opening Question: In "Self-Reliance," what is Emerson saying?

Core Questions: In paragraph one, what does Emerson want the reader to recognize?

Does he give men any advice?

What does he mean in paragraph three when he says, "Society everywhere is in conspiracy against the manhood of every one of its members"?

What would Emerson like to see in a man?

Closing Questions: Consider the people teens your age admire. How do they fit Emerson's definition of greatness?

Preseminar:

Task Description: At home, create a collage that illustrates the effects of peer pressure on yourself and other teens. Then, read "Self-Reliance" and define any vocabulary words you're unsure of (at least five or more words).

Time: Done as homework the evening before seminar; no time in class

Point Value: 25 points of seminar grade

Postseminar:

Task Description: Write an extended definition of *individualism*.

Time in class: None. All drafting will be done at home.

Format: Extended definition   Length: Four paragraphs

Point Value: 100 points of seminar score

Total seminar value: 200 points

FIGURE 7.26. PRESEMINAR TASK DESIGN ON "SELF-RELIANCE"

General Information:

A preseminar task is one component of the seminar process. This task, whatever it may be, is intended to cause the student to think deeply about the seminar selection before the discussion begins. The task also allows the facilitator to assess the student's reading readiness by concentrating on information the student should possess if he or she is prepared for seminar.

Suggested Preparation Activities:

1. As you read, mark your text for main ideas and interesting facts.
2. Keep a note sheet where you trace significant ideas through the selection.
3. Include page numbers for referencing the text.
4. Identify issues or questions you want to explore in the text.

Task:

1. Create a collage that illustrates the effects of peer pressure on yourself and other teens.
2. The size may vary, but it must be at least 8½×11.
3. Next, read Emerson's "Self-Reliance."
4. List and define five or more words from the essay. If you don't know the word, look it up. This must be turned in along with the collage.
5. Time: to be done at home prior to seminar date.

Assessment:

1. The preseminar task is worth 25 points of the seminar grade.
2. *Major focus* will be completion of both tasks. Collage will be graded for neatness, creativity, and originality.

FIGURE 7.27. POSTSEMINAR TASK DESIGN
ON "SELF-RELIANCE"

General Information:

A postseminar task is the final component of the seminar process. This task is designed to showcase what the participant has learned from reading, discussing, and analyzing the text. The length of the task and the point value of the task may vary.

Suggested Preparation Activities:

1. Review the notes you took during seminar.
2. Think about what each contributor said and the reasons for his or her position on the issues.
3. Think about issues that received superficial coverage in the seminar.

Task:

1. Write an extended definition of individualism.
2. Format: extended definition (see model and description).
3. Length: four paragraphs
4. Drafting: 2 drafts with the final draft done in blue or black ink or typed.
5. Time: All drafts to be completed as homework.

Assessment:

1. The postseminar task is worth 100 points of the total seminar grade (200 points).
2. Accuracy in grammar, spelling, usage, punctuation, and sentence structure are essential.
3. *Major focus* will be your content and the extended definition form.

Lesson design for seminar incorporates all principles of effective planning for the block schedule. Varied activities, specific expectations, and task design instruments for preseminar and postseminar are essential. Additionally, completing the teacher worksheet is an efficient method of planning seminars because all parts of the seminar process are addressed, and key questions are answered before the detailed task design work begins.

The final part of lesson planning and design is development of assessment instruments for each preseminar and postseminar task. Chapter 9, which discusses grading of seminars, includes both preseminar and postseminar assessment instruments for the four model lessons presented in this chapter.

Although the seminar can be conducted as an independent strategy, the process is much richer if all parts are included. Preseminar and postseminar activities prepare the reader, extend the learning, and pave the way for meaningful, less subjective assessment of seminars.

8

TROUBLESHOOTING THE "WHAT IFS..."

WHAT IF THE OPENING QUESTION IS ASKED AND NO ONE RESPONDS?

Healthy wait time is always appropriate after asking a good Socratic question. In fact, there often is a correlation between wait time and the quality of thought required by students before answering. Good teachers know what thinking looks like—students with eyes fixed on a distant point, a steadied stare at the ceiling with head and eyes alert, a tilt of the head and a wistful expression, a set, trance-like gaze on the mind's eye.

This thinking is not to be interrupted. The savvy teacher who detects the power of this question sits and waits, surveying the class, watching as first one and then others refer to their note references or begin to flip through the text. The wait may be as long as a couple of minutes. A soft and slow repeat of the question may be in order to resolidify the question, particularly if several look at the teacher for reassurance that they heard correctly.

In seminar, it is the students who should be uncomfortable with the silence, feeling obliged to fill the silence with their responses. The best advice on any question is to let the question "breathe" with generous wait time for student pondering.

If, however, the teacher reads blankness or confusion after asking a question, a rephrasing of the question may be in order to break it down more specifically. If this does not work, an alternative opening may help to jumpstart the discussion. In a seminar on Russell Baker's sardonic essay, "School Versus Education," the opening question was, "The terms 'school' and 'education' are often used interchangeably. Why does Baker set this up as 'school' *versus* 'education'?" The class sat there...forever! A repeat of the question drew only more fuzzy looks and head scratching. The teacher then backed away from the question's paradox and broke it into two consecutive questions. First, he asked, "What does Baker say schools are designed to do?" and the first core question was, "What does Baker have to say about one's education?" The class did much better with the irony when they explored each term first.

The toughest part of teacher preparation is to write questions that challenge and provoke, are broad and open-ended, and use language understood by all. For a ninth grade heterogeneous class reading "The Town Mouse and the Country Mouse," "What's going on between these mice?" beats "What platonic elements of friendship are explored in the rodents' interchange?" In the second question, the language barrier must be crossed before real thinking can begin for some students. The language of a question must be understood by the least able student in the room if all are to have equal access to the ideas of text.

When no one responds to the opening question, it may be that students have not read their text. Reading together, "qualifying" for seminar with a quiz or writing, and showing their notes or text marking are ways to guarantee that students arrive prepared. Bringing one's "ticket to the show" as evidence of preparation "admits" a student to seminar. This may be a public dropping of work into the teacher's hand as students enter the room. Our experience has been that students complete preseminar or qualifying work when they are slack on other assignments. Most do not want to be excluded from seminar and will do what it takes to be admitted.

However, qualifying for seminar may not be desirable as students are first introduced to the process and are not hooked on its power. Reading together or watching students read and complete preseminar task is the only guarantee that the reading has been completed. For beginning seminars, short, idea-laden pieces that can be read aloud or read in class ensure that the words have had air play prior to seminar. No seminar generally gets off the ground on any question unless the reading has occurred.

If students appear not to have read and speak in generalization without textual evidence, the teacher should end the seminar promptly. Continuing on this line is now counterproductive, and an alternative teaching strategy is needed. Simply pull out the "64 study questions." Students will likely prepare for seminar the next time!

WHAT IF SOME STUDENTS DO NOT "QUALIFY" FOR SEMINAR?

Teachers have several options for students who do not complete qualifying assignments. One option is to pass the students study questions on the reading to complete outside the door or across the hall in another teacher's room. Exclusion from the seminar circle and even from the classroom is an experience most do not want to repeat. If these options are not possible, students may work in a corner outside the circle; however, they often have difficulty concentrating since discussions are usually engaging. An arrangement with another teacher who uses the seminar for a spot in the back of that class is preferable. Another option is to have the student complete an outer circle task, in addition to submitting a replacement writing.

WHAT IF A STUDENT
MISBEHAVES DURING SEMINAR?

Because the most important factor in the success of the seminar strategy, next to guaranteeing that students have read the material, is that students feel safe, it is imperative that any behavioral breaches be swiftly addressed. If a student disagrees angrily, verbally attacking a classmate, the offender may be used as a learning example. The teacher could say, "Let me stop the seminar for a moment. John, what you said was a personal attack. Please restate your position civilly, disagreeing with her point, not with her. Thank you for letting me use you as an example for this rule." This recourse is used early in the process when students are still trying to "get it." Other options for addressing misbehavers are a "teacher look" or even a look followed by a thumb gesture indicating, "You're out." In this case, the meaning is "out of seminar" and translates as "pick up your study questions and go to another room for the remainder of seminar." A major infraction has just occurred!

Attention deficit students may need to flank the teacher in seminar so a gentle touch can redirect their fidgeting. They often choose the seat beside the teacher. Sometimes the class may be asked to vote on whether someone should be kicked out of seminar for insidious rule violations. This response is generally only needed once.

Some teachers establish seating charts for seminar days to ensure that students who would distract each other are not seated next to one another. These students, too, often engage in self-regulation, deciding to sit away from someone they might be tempted to distract or be distracted by.

WHAT IF ONE STUDENT TRIES
TO DOMINATE THE SEMINAR?

Overzealous speakers must be managed or the seminar is compromised. Because the seminar leader acknowledges each participant, a standing procedure can be always to recognize those who have not yet spoken before those who have, if several hands are up.

The talkative one also may "assist" the teacher by deliberately delaying his or her contribution until five classmates have responded to a question. This forces others to stop relying on the eager participant and allows all to practice reflecting longer before expressing a view.

Another useful strategy is to help an extroverted student focus on listening, not speaking, by placing this child in the outer circle with responsibility for listening and taking notes on the entire seminar. For the last few minutes of class, the student summarizes the seminar. This child certainly has his turn to speak, but his contribution is tempered by acute practice in listening, reflecting, and synthesizing—skills he may well need to develop!

WHAT IF SOME STUDENTS DO NOT SPEAK AT ALL DURING SEMINAR?

Many factors affect a child's willingness to speak. Naturally shy or insecure people will not speak easily until they are sure this is a "safe" place where no one is put down or otherwise judged for having a view. Gestures or words that mean "nerd," "goody two-shoes," or "teacher's pet" are often more destructive than those that say, "That's stupid." All are intolerable and should result in ejection from seminar every time! The rules, as previously discussed, must be strictly followed. This settles the mind and reduces the risk for reticent young people.

There always should be opportunity for those who do not speak in seminar to "make it up" in writing that night. This is a requirement for nonspeakers in the seminar and is called a "replacement writing" that is due the day following seminar. It is important that the teacher either assigns the topic(s) for writing or negotiates the topic(s) with the students. It is unacceptable to simply rehash the seminar they had the benefit of hearing the day before. Assigned topics will be ideas or issues not addressed in seminar so that no "free academic lunch" is consumed!

While there is no seminar if all choose the replacement writing option, it does provide an "out" for the painfully shy and for the natural introverts, who process information internally and often need more time to think before speaking. Natural extroverts, who process externally, figure out what they think by trying it out loud with other people. These students are first out of the blocks and get the seminar going. An hour later, the introvert has processed his thinking and may well make the most astute, well-substantiated comment of the seminar. As long as all have the option of writing for the seminar grade, the playing field is even for all personality types.

Several tricks often bring out reticent speakers. The round robin, moving one by one around the circle, may be used to solicit a response from those who have not yet contributed. A teacher may call on a student who has not asked for acknowledgment but who obviously has some ideas by asking, "Mark, did you have something?" This needed, yet gentle, invitation helps nudge the student through his shyness to test his voice.

WHAT IF SOME STUDENTS THINK OF THINGS AFTER SEMINAR THEY WISH THEY HAD SAID?

It should always be an option for students who speak in seminar but are dissatisfied with the degree to which they speak to enhance their seminar grade that evening with supplemental writing. Again, this contribution should add to, not replay, seminar ideas and must be submitted on the day following seminar.

Some will say *something* during seminar but may not be comfortable. Supplemental writing, as an option, allows them to test their voices without being locked into being graded during seminar only on what they say.

WHAT IF STUDENTS GO OFF ON A LINE OF REASONING THAT IS FAULTY OR INACCURATE AND START BUILDING ON IT?

The hope is that if an inaccuracy is voiced, another student will correct it. Because the teacher's role is not to judge outwardly, technical inaccuracies that are not built on should be allowed to pass. The teacher may note them and then correct them after the seminar. But if students develop dialogue around fallacies without dissent, the teacher may redirect the thinking with a follow-up question like, "Is there anyone who takes issue with this line of reasoning?" The teacher did not tell them they were on the wrong track; however, she did invite them to think about another side. This is often all it takes to have other views represented.

Another follow-up question, to call for evidence in text where none exists, should also short-circuit a faulty position. Occasionally, if these strategies do not work, the teacher may interrupt the seminar momentarily to establish facts before continuing with the seminar. This is only done if a key point, relevant for completion of the seminar, is incorrect, and subsequent discussion would be tainted without correction.

WHAT IF CLASS ENDS AND THE SEMINAR IS NOT FINISHED?

Teachers should monitor time closely during seminar to make some decision about what to do if time is running short. If the class is still exploring core questions, the teacher may wait for the current question to play itself out, then stop the seminar and announce that it will begin with a new question tomorrow and that nothing brought up today can be reintroduced.

If the cores are covered, the seminar's closing question can then become the post-seminar writing assignment, a response writing, or journal since its focus is personal relevance.

If time is short and part of tomorrow cannot be spared, the teacher may skip a couple of core, noting the need to "teach" these tomorrow, and move to the closing question. Students, and teachers for that matter, like the closure of a closing question. The sense of resolution or completion is more satisfying generally than having to end seminar *in medias res*.

WHAT IF SOME STUDENTS ARE ABSENT AND MISS A SEMINAR?

All students are accountable for a seminar grade, so absence is no excuse. Students may make up their seminar in a variety of ways. One option is for the student to come in before or after school for a one-on-one with the teacher, who asks perhaps the same or similar questions from the actual seminar. Two or three students may come in together for a three-on-one for an intense 10- to 15-minute seminar to explore their understanding.

Another option is for the student to submit an audiotape on either the teacher's seminar questions or topics from the reading that the student would like to address and which the teacher preapproves. Yet another way of accounting for the seminar is the submission of a replacement writing, again either on assigned or negotiated topics.

Teachers should note if a particular student seems to always be absent on seminar day. Occasionally, a student may try to dodge the seminar since it is "just a class discussion." The level of work that is required from such a miss, however, may soon eliminate the problem.

9

ASSESSMENT OF SEMINARS

Why grade seminars? Grading seminar identifies the strategy as more than a class discussion and as an integral part of the learning process. Routinely, students ask, "Is this going to count for a grade?" If the answer is "No," they perceive that preparation for the seminar is optional. Seminar is doomed as a learning strategy if this attitude exists. Students must be held accountable for their performances in seminar and for completion of the preseminar and postseminar tasks. In addition, students must be instructed on their responsibilities as participants and on grading procedures for all three parts of the seminar—preseminar, seminar, and postseminar. Students must be familiar with the seminar rubric and with all behavioral expectations. The teacher should model and explain exactly what he or she is looking for from participants. Additionally, students need to know how seminar will be weighted in the final averaging of grades.

While suggestions and pointers on grading can be given, the classroom teacher ultimately must design grading methods that best fit his class. There is one absolute in grading, however. No student's grade should be determined merely on the number of times he speaks! While one student may speak five times, another may speak only once yet contribute more significantly insightful information, or move the seminar into a new dimension. By using a rubric that targets the skill areas to be assessed (conduct, speaking, reasoning, listening, and reading), teachers and students alike are aware that excellence in seminar involves a multitude of behaviors and responsibilities. Design and grading instruments for the preseminar and postseminar tasks should give a clear description of these tasks and explain how they will be assessed. Because these tasks comprise a large portion of the seminar grade, students must know and understand all expectations before they begin the assignments.

For in-depth modeling of seminar planning, teachers should refer to the lesson designs of Chapter 7, which gives examples of planning worksheets and preseminar and postseminar design tasks. Unless teachers use a rubric to grade seminar, grading is somewhat subjective and indefensible. Use of rubrics makes grading of seminars more concrete, since grading is now based on stated exemplars and observable behaviors. More significantly, through use of the seminar rubric and preseminar and postseminar grading instruments, students are fully aware of how all parts of their seminar grade will be derived. For the teacher, grading is less stressful and more easily explained to students and parents because two parts of the grade are tangible, measurable tasks. The third segment—the seminar—is evaluated solely on the rubric, not on what the facilitator likes or dislikes. Objectivity in assessment is maintained.

RECORDING STUDENT BEHAVIORS

While conducting the seminar, the teacher must keep track of student responses and behaviors. After the seminar concludes, the data is then transferred to a score on the seminar rubric. Teachers have several options for tracking responses and behaviors. One method is to use charting symbols in combination with notes. Another method uses a checklist of observable behaviors where each behavior is marked as it occurs. Either technique works effectively, so teachers should use the method most comfortable to them.

CHARTING

Charting is a technique used by the facilitator to record what is actually occurring throughout the seminar. Symbols are used to indicate precisely what each participant has said or done. Charting is used after the seminar to assign the number of points earned by each student during the seminar. The facilitator also may elect to take notes on the comments made by each student.

Charting involves making notations or taking notes on students' participation during seminar. While having complete notes on students' comments is desirable, many teachers find the task overwhelming and must use symbols to denote established behaviors. Use of charting enables teachers to take targeted notes, such as objectives that are covered in seminar and objectives that must be covered in the next class session. For those who find the process of charting too demanding when listening is so critical, running an audiotape during the seminar and grading at a later time is a useful option.

These symbols could be used:

√ (student contributes)

9 (page number)

+ (clarification)

R (repetition)

P (paraphrase)

H (hitchhike)

These symbols may be combined to create a shorthand description of the student's behavior as follows:

√9+   Student makes a comment, cites a page, and draws a conclusion.

√9+   Student paraphrases and draws a conclusion.

√9+   Student makes a comment, cites a page, but does not draw a conclusion

√+   Student makes an insightful comment but does not quote from the text.

H9   Student hitchhikes or piggybacks on someone else's comment and quotes the text to clarify a peer's comment.

√–   Student gives his opinion and has no textual support; limited reasoning is evident.

√R–   Comment is made that has little thought involved or that is a repetition of someone else's comment; weak listening skills may be apparent.

√=   Student speaks just to get a grade.

Until the facilitator becomes adept at charting, he may choose to record the seminar on audiotape and play the tape back to assist in grading. Students need to be informed about how the tape will be used. Or, a teacher might ask another teacher for help with charting comments.

For charting and taking notes, a legal pad is best because space must be provided between student names to record information. For convenience, names are listed in the order students are seated within the circle. Charting on the teacher's pad might look something like this.

       ①   ②
Sue — √+ 18 new theme– revenge   √+ no documentation

         ①   ②
Barry — P+ 22 explained character's motives   R– repeated Rod's quote and inference

Charting is absolutely necessary because no teacher can fill out the rubric form for every student while the seminar is in progress. Charting allows the facilitator to focus on exemplars observed and make note of these behaviors. Later, immediately after the seminar ends if possible, these charting notes are transferred to the rubrics and a final score given. Charting notes are only for teacher's eyes; students have no need to see charting notes.

CHECKLISTS

Other teachers prefer using a grading checklist because it is cleaner to use. Also, for teachers who say leading seminars is demanding in itself without tossing grading into the mix, using the checklist is a way to make the task of grading more manageable and less confusing. Checklists enable teachers to break down the task to a comfortable level as they too gain competence in evaluation. One drawback, however, is that a checklist does not allow for detailed notes, which provide very specific information about each student.

The advanced checklist that is provided corresponds to rubric with all exemplars drawn from the excellence category. Beginning seminar participants have not mastered all these skills but are moving toward that goal. A blank checklist is also provided so that the teacher can list specific exemplars which are emphasized in each seminar. Teachers may start with as few as two exemplars from each assessment area and add more as the students progress and become more comfortable with seminar. Ideally, in each seminar students will be held accountable for additional exemplars until mastery is reached in each assessment area.

Yes, teachers must assess seminars if students are to value the learning strategy; however, instructors must also give themselves permission to break down assessment so that the process is manageable for their individual levels of competence as seminar leaders. holding students accountable for ten examples—two in each strand—is a good place to begin. For example, the seminar is worth 50 points of the grade. Now it's logical to assign 5 assessment points for each of the ten stated examples. Breaking the grading down in this way simplifies the process until the facilitator can handle looking at the entire rubric and assessing everything. Grading of seminars and informing students of the methodology is what is most important.

Figures 9.1 and 9.2 are grading checklists. Figure 9.1 (p. 134) is for use with the advanced student while Figure 9.2 (p. 136) is a blank form which requires the teacher to write in the exemplars for each use.

ASSIGNING POINT VALUES

Regardless of whether charting or checklists are used, teachers must transfer information to the rubric and assign point values for each student after the seminar ends. For instance, if the seminar is worth 50 points and two exemplars were stated in each assessment area, the teacher may ascribe 10 points for each area—conduct, speaking, listening, reading, and reasoning. Likewise, a 4 on the rubric indicates excellence, that all or most of the exemplars have been achieved. Whatever point value is assigned to the seminar, a bit of math is involved to determine how many points constitute an A or B. Converting the points to letter grades is easier for some teachers to manipulate, but certainly conversion is not necessary for all graders. The challenge of grading seminar is to decide specifically where the student falls on the rubric and then determine the points earned for that performance. Remember that two parts of the seminar remain—the preseminar and postseminar. These tasks are explicit assignments that get students energized and ready for seminar and later extend the learning. No grade is complete without all these parts.

Grading of seminars is difficult and somewhat controversial, and not all users of seminar agree on the need to grade. Some say that grading is too subjective, that only the preseminar and postseminar tasks should be scored. Others contend that not grading devalues the process as a teaching and learning tool.

Caught in this dilemma, the only reasonable option is to develop design and assessment instruments that are fair and more authentic grading procedures. Through regular use of these, both students and parents have a better understanding of expectations and grading methods.

ASSESSMENT MODELS

Figures 9.3 through 9.6 (pp. 138–141) are examples of preseminar and postseminar design and assessment instruments. Chapter 7 contains more lesson design models. The inclusion of preseminar and postseminar tasks here presents all graded parts of the seminar process in the order they are completed. In addition, the seminar rubric is included.

GRADING FEEDBACK

As teachers use the seminar rubric, each student should be given a copy during the preparation phase when students are taught the seminar process. While preseminar and postseminar tasks change with each seminar, the seminar rubric does not; consequently, a master copy of the rubric in each student's notebook is adequate. It is humanly impossible for teachers to fill out an individual rubric for each participant. Besides, the paper consumption itself would be staggering. Instead, each student receives a feedback sheet that identifies areas of strength and needed improvement for each of the three seminar components. At least one strength and improvement area should be targeted. Broader comments can be made at the bottom of the feedback form. The feedback sheet is not intended to be a duplication of the checklist or charting which are exclusively for teacher use. If students have additional questions, a quick conference usually suffices.

As soon as feasible after all three parts of the seminar are graded, teachers should return feedback sheets to students. In addition, conferencing with students on a regular basis in conjunction with the feedback is recommended. For many students, the exemplars are demanding. These students may need constant modeling and encouragement to achieve their best in seminar.

To assist teachers in managing paperwork, students should be asked to staple assessment forms to the preseminar and postseminar tasks as each is turned in. Also, students can fill out basic data on the seminar feedback sheet which will save the teacher valuable time. Figure 9.7 (p. 145) is an example of a feedback sheet for seminar.

(Text continues on page 146.)

FIGURE 9.1. ADVANCED GRADING CHECKLIST

Checklist of Observable Behaviors: Advanced Seminar Participant	Shows respect for seminar	Shows patience	Asks for clarification	Draws others into seminar	Move to new concepts	Exhibits self-control	Uses the hitchhike accurately	Speaks to all participants	Avoids talking too long	Speaks loud enough	Does not use slang/incorrect grammar	Articulates well	Has accurate pronunciation
STUDENT NAMES	CONDUCT							SPEAKING					

Understands question	Cites text for documentation	Relates and makes connections	Is logical and insightful	Does not piggy-back on errors	Considers all sources	Responds to student questions	Takes notes	Avoids repetition	Builds on peers' comments	Points out flawed reasoning	Overcomes distractions	Can pass a quiz	Can quickly locate reference	Has marked the text	Understands major concepts	Identifies contradictions	Scale: Strong ✓ + Average ✓ Weak ✓ – Not at all –
REASONING						LISTENING						READING					POINTS EARNED

FIGURE 9.2. BLANK GRADING CHECKLIST

Checklist of Observable Behaviors:						
STUDENT NAMES	CONDUCT			SPEAKING		

									Scale: Strong ✓ + Average ✓ Weak ✓ − Not at all −
REASONING			LISTENING			READING			POINTS EARNED

FIGURE 9.3. TASK DESIGN FOR PRESEMINAR ON PLATO'S *APOLOGY*

General Information:

A preseminar task is the first component in the seminar process. This task, whatever it may be, is intended to cause the student to think deeply about the seminar selection before the discussion begins. The task also allows the facilitator to assess the student's reading readiness by concentrating on information the student should possess if he or she is prepared for seminar.

Suggested Preparation Activities:

1. As you read, mark your text for main ideas and interesting facts.
2. Keep a note sheet where you trace significant ideas throughout the selection. Include page numbers.
3. Identify ideas that you want to explore in the seminar.

Task:

1. You are to write for 20 minutes on Plato's *Apology*.
2. The form of the writing should be an extended paragraph supporting this topic sentence:

    Socrates was on trial because _____.

3. Give at least three reasons and an explanation of why he may have been on trial.
4. Conclude with a clincher sentence that pulls your response together.

Assessment:

1. This writing is worth 20 points of the total seminar grade.
2. All elements of proper paragraph writing will be assessed: topic sentence, supporting details, elaboration of ideas, and drawing a concluding inference.
3. Punctuation, spelling, sentence structure, and usage also are assessed.
4. *Major focus* will be your ability to answer the question of why Socrates was on trial and to give evidence from the text for support.
5. The writer must observe the time limits but may use the text.

**FIGURE 9.4 TASK DESIGN FOR POSTSEMINAR
ON PLATO'S *APOLOGY***

General Information:

A postseminar task is the third component of the seminar process. This task is designed to showcase what the seminar participant has learned from reading, discussing, and analyzing the text. The length of the task and the point value of the task may vary.

Suggested Preparation Activities:

1. Review the notes you took during the seminar.
2. Think about what each contributor said and the reasons for his or her position on issues.
3. Think about issues that received superficial coverage in the seminar.

Task:

1. You are to write a response essay reflecting on what characteristics of Socrates you would like to possess in your own life.
2. The form of writing should be four or five paragraphs.
   a. The introduction should hook the reader, state the source, and present the thesis statement.
   b. Each body paragraph should explore a characteristic of Socrates that you want to have. State the characteristic and elaborate fully.
   c. The concluding paragraph should redirect attention on Socrates as an admirable character who has qualities worthy of possessing in a modern society.
3. Purpose: to explain and to reflect.
4. Point of view: first person.
5. Tone: Formal, standard English.

Assessment:

1. Total point value for seminar: 30 points.
2. Major focuses: essay writing form, elaboration of ideas, punctuation, usage, spelling, sentence structure, and originality of thinking.

FIGURE 9.5. ASSESSMENT INSTRUMENTS FOR PRESEMINAR AND POSTSEMINAR ON PLATO'S *APOLOGY*

PRESEMINAR ASSESSMENT:

Points Earned:

1. Form: Topic sentence—5 points   _____

              Each supporting reason—
                 2 points each (6)   _____

              Elaboration of reasons—
                 1 point each (3)   _____

              Clincher sentence (inference)—1   _____

2. Accuracy of punctuation and usage: 5 points   _____

3. TOTAL NUMBER OF POINTS EARNED: (20)   _____

POSTSEMINAR ASSESSMENT:

Points Earned:

1. Essay form (15)   _____
   a. Paragraphing and sentence style
   b. Thesis statement
   c. Elaboration of reasons
   d. Coherence and unity

2. Grammatical and mechanical accuracy (5)   _____
   a. Spelling
   b. Usage
   c. Punctuation

3. Originality and depth of thought (5)   _____
   a. Factual accuracy
   b. Relevance to yourself

4. Point of view (3)   _____

5. Tone (2)   _____

6. TOTAL NUMBER OF POINTS EARNED: _____

TOTALS

_____ Preseminar (20)
_____ Seminar (50)
_____ Postseminar (30)
_____ FINAL SEMINAR GRADE

FIGURE 9.6. SEMINAR RUBRIC

Student_____ Grader _____

Date _____   Topic _____

Directions: Identify the descriptors that best reflect the student's performance in each of the five areas.

(A) Conduct: ____   (B) Speaking: ____   (C) Reasoning: ____

(D) Listening: ____   (E) Reading: ____   *Total Points* ____

Scale: **Excellent 4;   Good 3;   Fair 2; Unsatisfactory 1**

Conduct:

4
- Demonstrates clear respect for the learning process
- Exhibits patience with differing opinions and thought complexity
- Shows initiative by asking peers for clarification
- Attempts to draw others into the discussion
- Moves forward onto new concepts
- Recognizes his or her own nit-picking and avoids it
- Does not gain attention by inappropriate means
- Exhibits control of potentially hurtful nonverbal behaviors
- Uses the hitchhike symbol sparingly

3
- Shows composure but may sometimes show slight impatience
- Is not impatient while waiting to be recognized to speak
- Demonstrates a respectful attitude towards others
- May comment frequently but makes no attempt to involve others
- Shows a desire to contribute responsibility to the seminar

2
- Participates verbally but shows impatience with seminar process
- May make insightful comments but does so sparingly
- May be argumentative and generally lacks poise
- May be unfocused because of depth or length of seminar

1
- Shows no respect for the learning environment
- Is argumentative and rude
- Takes advantage of or causes distractions
- Arrives unprepared with text, paper, or pen
- Wants the floor for himself and not to further the seminar
- Is writing personal notes instead of seminar notes
- May actually attempt to sleep during the discussion

Speaking:

4   • Speaks to all participants, not just to the facilitator
       • Avoids the urge to talk too long
       • Speaks loudly enough to be heard by all
       • Avoids using slang and incorrect grammar
       • Articulates clearly and precisely
       • Pronounces words accurately and appears to know meanings

3   • Addresses the majority of comments to peers, not the leader
       • Attempts to move the conversation onto a new idea
       • Does not try to say "everything" while he is recognized
       • Tries to speak louder when signaled to do so
       • May mumble or stumble over unfamiliar words but does so
         sparingly

2   • Speaks directly to teacher
       • Speaks too softly and needs to be reminded to speak louder
       • Routinely lapses into use of slang or substandard usage
       • Cannot pronounce key words in the text
       • Speaks only with prompting and has no sustainable point

1   • Is reluctant to speak when called on or passes in "round robin"
       • Mumbles and mispronounces words
       • Cannot be heard at all
       • Shows absolutely no desire to contribute verbally

Reasoning:

4   • Understands the question that has been posed before answering
       • Cites logical, relevant textual passages to support views
       • Relates the reading to other readings or studies
       • Expresses thoughts in complete sentences
       • Adds to the seminar significantly with insightful comments
       • Makes connections between own thoughts and those of others
       • Resolves contradictory ides of self and peers
       • Considers all sources, not just his or her own
       • Avoids piggy-backing on inaccuracies

3   • Responds to questions without any prompting
       • Demonstrates some reflection on the text but not mastery of it
       • Can make limited connections with ideas of other speakers
       • Can somewhat relate own ideas to other readings or seminars
       • Uses quotes or paraphrases but inferences are underdeveloped
       • Makes comments that are intriguing enough to merit reaction

2
- May have read the text but has not thought about it before seminar
- May overlook important points, thus leading to faulty logic
- May be accurate on minor points while missing the main concept
- Contributes opinions that have no textual support for them
- Has some difficulty in formulating understandable comments

1
- Makes illogical comments
- Says no more than "I agree"
- Ignores previous comments and directional movement of the seminar
- Attempts to use humor to avoid having to do serious thinking

Listening:

4
- Listens for opportunities to respond to student-generated questions
- Does not overlook details
- Writes down questions, comments, or ideas
- Avoids repetition or previous remarks of self and peers
- Builds on and acknowledges what other participants have said
- Points out flawed reasoning
- Overcomes any distractions

3
- Is generally attentive and focused
- Responds thoughtfully to ideas and questions that are raised
- May be too absorbed with own thoughts to hear others' comments
- May write down some thoughts, though does not consistently do so

2
- Responds only to ideas that are personally interesting
- Asks for repetition of questions or for rephrasing of questions
- Takes very limited notes
- May be easily distracted or may be the source of distraction
- Does not look up the text as it is cited by another student
- Does not visibly respond to cited text; may be unaware of location

1
- Is inattentive to other speakers
- Exhibits the body language: "I'd rather be anywhere but here."
- Makes comments that show total misinterpretation of material
- May not listen well enough to understand points of others
- Takes no notes during the seminar

Reading:

4
- Passes a reading comprehension test
- Is familiar with the text and can quickly locate quotations
- Has marked the text or has a note sheet
- Understands major concepts in the reading
- Identifies any contradictions in the reading

3
- Passes a reading comprehension quiz
- Has marked the text or prepared notes
- Can locate most references in the text when needed
- Demonstrates knowledge of facts, but may lack mastery of concepts
- Acknowledges difficulty with reading and asks for clarification

2
- Knows minimum on quiz
- Has little or no marking of text and has scanty notes
- Is confused about key concepts because of hasty reading
- Makes comments that reflect shallow knowledge of first few pages

1
- Is clearly unprepared and fails reading quiz
- Is unfamiliar with the text
- Has no notes or marking of text
- Asks for no help with the reading

FIGURE 9.7. SEMINAR REACTION AND DATA SHEET

STUDENT _____   DATE _____

SEMINAR TITLE _____

PRESEMINAR: Points earned _____

Strength:

Areas of Needed Improvement:

SEMINAR: Points earned _____

Strength:

Areas of Needed Improvement:

POSTSEMINAR: Points earned _____

Strengths:

Areas of Needed Improvement:

TOTAL SCORE: _____

SUGGESTION FOR OVERALL IMPROVEMENT:

ASSESSMENT OF PRESEMINARS AND POSTSEMINARS

Another part of assessment is determining point values for each component of seminar. The depth of tasks, time required to complete them, and objectives realized from doing the tasks often determine their point value. Similarly, the time spent in seminar and the intensity of the piece affect the value. Undoubtedly, a one-page reading will not be assigned as many points as an entire novel that has been time consuming for students in reading preparation and in preseminar and postseminar tasks. Point value must be assigned so students are rewarded for every activity. This includes any directed reading assignments, outer circle tasks, and the three components of seminar. No part of preparation should be ignored in the grading process. The following are point value breakdowns for each part of seminar:

- ◆ For a novel or longer paired readings
  - Preseminar 50
  - Seminar 100
  - Postseminar 50
- ◆ For seminar where tasks are done in class before and after seminar
  - Preseminar 25
  - Seminar 50
  - Postseminar 25
- ◆ For the most demanding reading and tasks
  - Preseminar 100
  - Seminar 100
  - Postseminar 100

In discussing lesson design for seminars in Chapter 7, four model lessons were included; however, the assessments of the preseminar and postseminar tasks were not. The next four figures are sample assessments for those tasks.

FIGURE 9.8. PRESEMINAR AND POSTSEMINAR ASSESSMENT INSTRUMENTS: "THIS SACRED SOIL" (P. 100)

PRESEMINAR ASSESSMENT:

____ 1. Content (15)

    a. Selection of films, television shows, or literature

    b. Explanations of portrayals

    c. Personal reactions

____ 2. Format (10)

    a. Includes introduction, body, and conclusion

    b. Length is adequate.

    c. Point of view is first person.

____ 3. Editing (5)

____ Total points earned of possible 30.

POSTSEMINAR ASSESSMENT:

____ 1. Content (10)

    a. Understanding of Native American beliefs and practices

    b. Logical applications to modern society

____ 2. Format (5)

    a. Extended paragraph

    b. Includes all elements of paragraphing

____ 3. Editing (5)

____ Total points earned of possible 20.

FIGURE 9.9. PRESEMINAR AND POSTSEMINAR ASSESSMENT INSTRUMENTS: "THE FROGS DESIRING A KING" (P. 106)

PRESEMINAR:

____ 1. Detailed completion of graphic organizer (5)

____ 2. Content—depth and logic of argument (10)

____ 3. Form—complete sentences (5)

____ Total points earned of possible 20

POSTSEMINAR:

____ 1. Purpose (5)

____ 2. Tone—serious, academic (5)

____ 3. Structure (15)
   a. Introduction and clear thesis
   b. Body—2 or more paragraphs
   c. Conclusion

____ 4. Drafting (15)
   a. At least two drafts
   b. Evidence of revision on final draft
   c. Final draft in ink or typed

____ 5. Editing—accuracy in spelling, punctuation, sentence structure, usage, and grammar (10)

____ Total points earned of possible 50

FIGURE 9.10. PRESEMINAR AND POSTSEMINAR ASSESSMENT INSTRUMENTS: "A PSALM OF LIFE" (P. 111)

PRESEMINAR:

____ 1. Completion of task—lyrics and poster (10)

____ 2. Time on task in group activity (10)

____ Total points earned of possible 20

POSTSEMINAR:

____ 1. Content–contains attitudes and aspirations (15)

____ 2. Format—lyric poem of 3 or more stanzas (10)

____ 3. Drafting—2 drafts with final in ink (10)

____ 4. Editing—accuracy in spelling, punctuation (5)

____ Total points earned of possible 40.

FIGURE 9.11. PRESEMINAR AND POSTSEMINAR ASSESSMENT INSTRUMENTS: "SELF-RELIANCE" (P. 116)

PRESEMINAR:

____ 1. Collage—neatness, creativity, and originality (15)

____ 2. Vocabulary—unfamiliar words are defined (10)

____ Total points earned of possible 25

POSTSEMINAR: EXTENDED DEFINITION RUBRIC

____ 1. Format (15)
   a. Four paragraphs
   b. Meets design guidelines

____ 2. Content (30)
   a. Strong, captivating introduction
   b. Effective vocabulary and sentence style

____ 3. Drafting (35)
   a. Prewriting notes (5)
   b. Initial draft (10)
   c. Polished final draft (20)

____ 4. Revision and Editing: (20)
   a. Accuracy in spelling, punctuation, grammar, and usage
   b. Effective sentence structures

____ Total points earned of possible 100

GRADING CHALLENGES AND WRAPUP

"How do I assess students who are absent on seminar day?" Yes, these students must be held accountable for the work they have missed by doing a "replacement" task. Several options are available—the student can be given the seminar questions to which he responds in writing; the student may record his thoughts on an audiotape; or the student may conference after school with the teacher. Each option holds the student responsible for the seminar discussion and for preseminar and postseminar tasks.

"What about that student who says nothing during the seminar?" Perhaps this student is an introverted thinker who needs to hear and process everything before he speaks. For this student, "supplemental" writing is permitted if the writing is submitted at the next class session and does not summarize the seminar. Supplemental writing should cover entirely new information that was not discussed during seminar. Most teachers refuse to give full point value to supplemental writing since the student was present during seminar. The goal is to get the student talking!

Assessment of seminar is essential if students are to value it. While they may enjoy the process tremendously without it being assessed, students will not have consistent intensity or preparation. As a teaching strategy, the instructor must know that goals are being met through the seminar, as evidenced by the exemplars from the seminar rubric. When these behaviors are observable during seminar, and when preseminar and postseminar tasks show growth and knowledge, the seminar process is an effective teaching tool.

Regardless of how many grading models are given, no teacher can become competent in grading without consistent practice and refinement of skills. Certainly, rubrics are a tremendous aid for making grading more concrete; however, one must gain experience in using them successfully. Grading a seminar cannot ever be as rote as scoring an objective test because there are far too many variables to consider. Likewise, explanations on grading of seminars will always lack specificity because stating grading absolutes is neither possible nor desirable. Through use of rubrics, however, grading seminars is not unlike assessing compositions or other authentic tasks where students demonstrate what they know and can do. For the teacher, all this takes practice and familiarity with the rubric.

Finally, teachers should never be satisfied with a seminar unless they themselves learn something new and surprising. That's when teachers truly become "the guide on the side" and not "the sage on the stage."

10

PROFESSIONAL EVALUATION AND COACHING FOR SEMINAR

A few years ago, an assistant principal was busily making the rounds of observing and evaluating teachers when he stopped by for an unannounced observation of a teacher who was in the middle of a seminar. He walked in, never having witnessed the seminar before, took a seat, got out his pen and forms, and began to look and listen. He made very few notes and appeared puzzled though pleased with what he was hearing. After 10 minutes or so, he quietly got up, made eye contact with the teacher and mouthed these words, "This is good, but I'll come back sometime when you're teaching."

For the "unenlightened" principal or evaluator, seminar may not seem to fit neatly onto a district evaluation instrument. Teachers often report that a perceived obstacle to using the seminar strategy is that it is somehow incompatible with their teacher performance appraisal instruments. These teachers indicate, therefore, that they are unlikely to use the seminar when being evaluated.

While it may involve some thinking outside the box, a seminar, as an observable act, and a conference on accompanying pre- and post seminar activities *do* provide, for most evaluative instruments, sufficient evidence for a teacher evaluation.

Figure 10.1 uses language common to many evaluative instruments and cites sample evidence which may be observed or submitted with Socratic Seminar.

FIGURE 10.1. TEACHER PERFORMANCE APPRAISAL USING SOCRATIC SEMINAR

Management of Instructional Time:

	√	−

- ◆ Materials are ready and class starts promptly.
  - Did students move quickly to the circle?
  - Did teacher have charting and other record-keeping materials out and ready?
- ◆ Students get on task quickly and maintain a high task focus.
  - Did the teacher focus students on the reading for a moment as soon as all were in the circle?
  - Did students respond to teacher questions?
  - Were there multiple responses (6+) for each teacher question?
  - Did students ask questions, reference their peers, add to or otherwise respond, taking into consideration the contributions of their peers?
  - Did student affect indicate attention, interest, and responsibility for the task?

Management of Student Behavior:

	√	−

- ◆ Rules for participation, movement, and administrative matters are evident.
  - Do students speak only after recognition from the teacher?
  - Do students address their comment to their peers primarily?
  - Do students keep all comments public, with no side conversations?
  - Are all students respectful to their peers in both their body language and words?
- ◆ Behaviors are frequently monitored and inappropriateness is stopped.
  - Does the teacher frequently scan the circle to check for hands, behavior, and body expressions?
  - Does the teacher address every breach of protocol from a student speaking out of turn or talking with a neigh-

bor, to interrupting or putting someone down with words or body language?

Instructional Monitoring

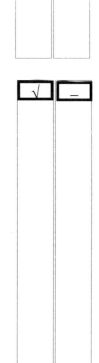

- ◆ Deadlines and performance standards are in place.
    - Did students quote or paraphrase from text in defending point of view?
    - Does the teacher pose a few potent, thoughtful questions?
    - Did the teacher ask followup questions when students did not defend a position or when they made generalizations?
    - Does the teacher take notes and transfer them to a student feedback sheet and grade?
- ◆ Written work products are used to check progress.
    - Was a preseminar assignment collected or reviewed?
    - Was a postseminar assignment made?

The teacher circulates to check student performance.

- Does the teacher set up an order for responses when several hands are up?
- Does the teacher scan the circle for students who appear to have comments?

Instructional Feedback

- ◆ Prompt affirming and sustaining feedback is provided for student answers.
    - Does the teacher return a feedback sheet within two to three class periods after seminar?
    - Does the teacher record student comments?
    - Does the teacher maintain neutral body language?
    - Does the teacher refuse to offer comments on anything during seminar?
    - Does the teacher limit talk to a few direct questions and an occasional followup question?
    - Does the teacher follow the seminar with a debriefing of how they did (i.e., a comparison of ideas and issues sheet with ones marked off after seminar)?

Instructional Presentation

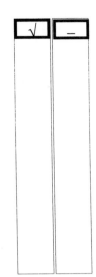

- ◆ Teacher uses eye contact, fluent language, wait time, and appropriate levels of questions.
  - Does the teacher follow the order of question type—opening, core, and closing?
  - Are the questions compelling and thought-provoking?
  - Do the questions tap complexity, ambiguity, controversy?
  - Are the questions free of values or judgment words?
  - Does the teacher tolerate the anxiety of silence (generous wait time) after asking a question or in between student comments?

Comments:

Management of Instructional Time:

Management of Student Behavior:

Instructional Monitoring

Instructional Feedback

Instructional Presentation

In the first three areas (instructional time, student behavior, and instructional monitoring), the transfer of skills from a regular class discussion to the seminar is fairly simple. The models tend to fit. However, the shift in thinking occurs in the feedback loop because all feedback in seminar is from the students' peers unless the teacher asks a followup question. However, the subset of skills in the feedback area for teachers doing seminar is very specific; it is primarily the absence of the attributes that makes a good leader.

The only teaching area that really cannot be assessed traditionally in a seminar is instructional presentation because the teacher is limited to a few questions to establish what the students have already figured out or what they deduce as they listen to and talk with peers. The evaluator need only stop by after seminar or the following day to see what will be taught more directly because the teacher will only cover items not fully addressed in seminar.

Yet another role principals, department heads, or mentors may play is as a peer coach for a teacher who is practicing the seminar. While some questions from the instructional presentation set may be difficult to assess without specific training in Socratic Seminar, many of the rest, particularly for another teacher who has been trained and is using the strategy, may be questions on which the teacher may like feedback. The best peer-coaching models are set up to provide nonjudgmental feedback on issues or observations the teacher himself desires.

Figure 10.2. is a checklist that may be used for peer coaching even when the coach has little or no experience with seminar. With limited dialogue, a peer or an evaluator could monitor the presence or absence of a set of teacher behaviors that should be evident in every seminar.

FIGURE 10.2. SELF-ASSESSMENT INSTRUMENT
FOR SEMINAR LEADER OR PEER COACH

Yes   No

_____   _____   1. Teacher collected preseminar assignments before beginning the seminar

_____   _____   2. Teacher asked for a moment of silence to allow students to block out extraneous conversations and to focus on the text.

_____   _____   3. Teacher had all charting and record keeping materials ready.

_____   _____   4. Teacher reminded students of at least one rule and one expectation before asking the opening question.

_____   _____   5. Teacher was seated on the same level as students.

_____   _____   6. Teacher refrained from giving his or her own opinion (words and gestures).

_____   _____   7. Teacher stated the opening question in clear and simple language.

_____   _____   8. Teacher asked followup and clarification questions.

_____   _____   9. Teacher listened well to students and allowed his or her questions to build on a student comment.

_____   _____   10. Teacher was comfortable with silence and allowed for wait time.

_____   _____   11. Teacher called on all students, recognizing new participants before calling on those who had already spoken.

_____   _____   12. Teacher firmly but gently corrected misbehavior by restating seminar rules.

_____   _____   13. Teacher spoke infrequently and then only briefly, thereby enabling students to feel in control of their seminar.

_____   _____   14. Teacher, by example, created an atmosphere of trust and respect.

_____   _____   15. Teacher clearly explained the requirements of the postseminar task and stated his or her expectations.

Used together, the Performance Appraisal (Fig. 10.1) and Self-Assessment Instrument (Fig. 10.2) provide a cursory "bottom line" introduction to seminar skills for evaluators. Principals evaluate the French teacher in a level III class without knowing how to speak a word of French. The skills of good practice are evident without knowing the language. By the same token, most evaluation instruments document practices that are evident in most classes, except that some of these practices occur in unique ways through Socratic Seminar.

Ideally, principals should understand both the philosophy behind a Socratic discussion and the specifics of leading it well. Otherwise, teachers may embrace an exciting and powerful alternative to class discussions that they must relegate to the closet if a principal comes to evaluate.

Principals and other teacher evaluators would benefit both from training in and reading about Socratic Seminar. They may also work with teachers who use the strategy to align exemplary seminar behaviors with those criteria adopted by the district for teacher performance appraisal. In most cases, the values codified in district performance instruments exist through the seminar and its pre- and postassignments.

A dialogue between teachers and evaluators to establish these links may be sufficient for savvy administrators to judge teacher performance when a seminar is the lesson plan. Surely, watching highly engaged students discuss text and being the sense makers for 97% of the class period is preferable to watching the teacher do the same. District or school instruments should not be a barrier to using an effective strategy. And isn't that a great part of a district or principal's mission—the removal of barriers so teachers can best work effectively with students?

THE BOTTOM LINE

While Socratic seminars are manageable in any school structure, they offer schools with longer blocks of uninterrupted time a more natural and effective strategy for extended discussion. It is neither a simple nor entirely predictable strategy to facilitate when students are "on," speaking 97% of class time.

Leading Socratic Seminars is somewhat akin to fly-fishing. The teacher throws out a question and floats the line, seeking a wide range of comments and evidences by students. Discussion may resemble Faulkner's stream of consciousness as one speaker's thoughts follow another, not always logically, but always moving, doubling back, subject to the prevailing winds. But then the fly fisherman reels in, tightens the slack by asking a followup question or returning to the original question. He pulls the line to the right or left with another core question and casts again with a closing question.

This is the skill of the bass master and the seminar leader. What they do looks easy, even effortless. It takes energy, intuitive listening, lots of practice and even a little faith to do it well. And the beneficiaries? Our "fish" are hungry. The pond is fully stocked. We need only have the proper bait and skilled fishermen to get them hooked. Socratic Seminars are proving to be a most potent lure!

Finally, no teacher should assume that reading about how to conduct seminars is sufficient. That's comparable to a doctor performing heart surgery without ever having seen surgery or practiced it. Teachers need to attend workshops where they can practice leading seminars and have their questions answered by an experienced facilitator. Although seminar models may be useful, they cannot substitute for practice.

BIBLIOGRAPHY

REFERENCES

Adler, M. J. (1982; 1984). *The Paideia Proposal*. New York: Macmillian.

Adler, M. J., and Van Doren, C. (1972). *How to Read a Book*. New York: Simon & Schuster.

Armstrong, T. (1998). *Awakening Genius in the Classroom*. Alexandria, VA: ASCD.

Dunn, R., and Dunn, K. (1992). *Teaching Secondary Student Through Their Individual Learning Syles*. Allyn & Bacon.

OTHER SOURCES

Adler, M. J. (1983). *How to Speak, How to Listen*. New York: Macmillian.

Briggs, I. M. (1980). *Gifts Differing*. Palo Alto, CA: Consulting Psychologists Press.

Goodlad, J. I. (1984). *A Place Called School*. New York: McGraw.

Kohn, K. (1993). *Punished by Rewards: The Trouble With Gold Stars, Incentive Plans, A's, Praise, and Other Bribes*. Boston: Houghton Mifflin.

North Carolina Education Standards and Accountability Commission (1995). Second Annual Report to General Assembly

Sylvester, R. (1995). *A Celebration of Neurons: An Educators Guide to the Human Brain*. Alexandria, VA: ASCD.

Weiss, P. F. (1987). *Great Ideas: A Seminar Approach to Teaching and Learning*. Chicago: Encyclopedia Britannica.